Mapping and Monitoring
Bullying and Violence

Mapping and Monitoring Bullying and Violence

Building a Safe School Climate

Ron Avi Astor

AND

Rami Benbenishty

OXFORD
UNIVERSITY PRESS

Oxford University Press is a department of the University of Oxford. It furthers the University's objective of excellence in research, scholarship, and education by publishing worldwide. Oxford is a registered trade mark of Oxford University Press in the UK and certain other countries.

Published in the United States of America by Oxford University Press
198 Madison Avenue, New York, NY 10016, United States of America.

CIP data is on file at the Library of Congress
ISBN 978-0-19-084706-7

9 8 7 6 5 4 3 2

Printed by Sheridan Books, Inc., United States of America

This publication was developed by the USC *Welcoming Practices* team in conjunction with the *Welcoming Practices* consortium of school districts, in part, with grant funds from the U.S. Department of Defense Educational Activity (DoDEA) under award # HE125420130260248. The views expressed do not necessarily reflect the positions or policies of the DoDEA, and no official endorsement by DoDEA is intended or should be inferred.

A portion of royalties will be donated by each of the authors to educational causes related to the topics covered in the book.

Contents

Foreword

Dorothy Espelage

Despite widespread efforts to make schools safer, school violence remains a national concern in the United States (Zhang, Musu-Gillette, & Oudekerk, 2016). School violence, bullying, aggression, and peer victimization are best understood from an ecological perspective in which individual characteristics of children interact with environmental systems (e.g., families, peers, schools, etc.) that in turn promote or deter victimization and perpetration (Espelage, 2014; Hong & Espelage, 2012). While this framework has been used to explore the risk and protective factors associated with violence, it is rarely adopted comprehensively to prevent school safety concerns. More specifically, school safety initiatives are often narrowly focused on school security measures (e.g., detectors, cameras, security officers), threat assessment trainings, and punitive disciplinary methods. Although these approaches are necessary to promote physical safety, they are simply insufficient in several significant ways. They do not necessarily address the emotional safety concerns of teachers and students, they do not give "voice" to all school community members (e.g., students, teachers, parents, administrators), and they do not promote the trust among individuals that is needed to promote school safety in a sustainable fashion.

In stark contrast, this book, Mapping and Monitoring Bullying and Violence: Building a Safe School Climate by Astor and Benbenishty, demonstrates beautifully how the social-ecological framework can be used to promote emotional and physical safety, to give voice to all school community members, and to promote positive school environments. As a scholar-practitioner who interacts with students, families, administrators, and teachers in K-12 settings on a regular basis, I am aware of the challenges of approaching school safety issues through a comprehensive approach as outlined in this book. However, Astor and Benbenishty provide a practical, data-driven approach that can be easily implemented. They provide clear and concrete guidance on how school districts can leverage current data systems with other types of data, including focus groups, surveys, observations, and mapping procedures to gather information across different components of the school ecological system.

Furthermore, their focus on social-emotional learning (SEL) in the context of data gathering and monitoring represents a sharp departure from many school safety approaches. Indeed, many schools are using SEL approaches to promote SEL competencies such as self-awareness, self-management, social awareness, relationship skills, and responsible decision-making (see http://www.casel.org/core-competencies/). These programs boost students' capacity to build positive relationships with peers and adults and to prevent aggression and victimization.

But data collection and SEL approaches are likely to be most beneficial when the climate in classrooms, schools, and communities is addressed. Astor and Benbenishty's innovative approach to school safety recognizes that when teachers and students perceive a positive school climate, there is less bullying and aggression, greater equity, and traditionally marginalized students feel safer (Espelage, Polanin, & Low, 2015; Rinehart & Espelage, 2016). Interestingly, Thapa, Cohen, Guffey, and Higgins-D'Alessandro (2013), in a review of more than 200 studies, identified four essential components of school climate: safety, relationships, teaching and learning, and institutional environment. Astor and Benbenishty's monitoring and mapping approach assesses all dimensions through multiple informants and multiple methods without overwhelming school representatives charged with promoting school safety.

Taken together, this book provides clear guidance for schools to address bullying, school climate, and emotional and physical safety through data monitoring, mapping, and SEL approaches. The authors recognize the importance of providing all school community members with opportunities to communicate their perceptions of school safety. This approach takes decades of research and partnerships with schools both nationally and internationally and creates a comprehensive, step-by-step approach that engages all stakeholders.

Dorothy Espelage, Ph.D.
Professor, University of Florida

REFERENCES

Espelage, D. L. (2014). Ecological theory: Preventing youth bullying, aggression, & victimization. *Theory into Practice, 53,* 257–264.

Espelage, D. L., Polanin, J., & Low, S. (2014). Teacher and staff perceptions of school environment as predictors of student aggression, victimization, and willingness to intervene in bullying situations. *School Psychology Quarterly, 29* (3), 387–405. doi: 10.1080/00405841.2014.947216

Espelage, D. L., Van Ryzin, M., & Holt, M. K. (2017). Trajectories of bully perpetration across early adolescence: Static risk factors, dynamic covariates and longitudinal outcomes. *Psychology of Violence.* Online first.

Hong, J. S., & Espelage, D. L. (2012). A review of research on bullying and peer victimization in school: An ecological systems analysis. *Aggression and Violent Behavior, 17,* 311–312. doi: 10.1016/j.avb.2012.03.003.

Rinehart, S. J., & Espelage, D. L. (2016). School level predictors of homophobic name-calling & sexual harassment victimization/perpetration among middle school youth. *Psychology of Violence, 6,* 213–222. doi: 10.1037/a0039095

Thapa, A., Cohen, J., Guffey, S., & Higgins-D'Alessandro, A. (2013). A review of school climate research. *Review of Educational Research, 83,* 357–385. doi: 10.3102/0034654313483907

Zhang, A., Musu–Gillette, L., & Oudekerk, B. A. (2016). *Indicators of school crime and safety: 2015* (NCES 2016-079/NCJ 249758). Washington, DC: National Center for Education Statistics, U.S. Department of Education, and Bureau of Justice Statistics, Office of Justice Programs, U.S. Department of Justice.

Acknowledgments

This guide is the outcome of a very long and productive personal and intellectual friendship between the authors. As such, it reflects our learning from so many partners, too numerous to name, along the way.

We'd like to thank our respective universities that supported this work, mainly, USC and Bar Ilan University in the most recent decade. Our many former and current students and colleagues have challenged us and help sharpen our ideas.

We thank all our partners around the world who helped us see what is shared by all educational settings, as well as the uniqueness of each and every school and student. We are particularly indebted to our partners in Israel, Chile, and France. Special thanks to the educators and colleagues in the cities of Herzelya, Givaatayem, and Valparaiso, and to professionals in the Israeli and Chilean ministries of education who partnered with us in creating monitoring systems.

In the United States, we thank the *Building Capacity* and *Welcoming Practices* consortiums whose more than 145 schools were the source of many of the examples in this book. The superintendents, school boards, district administrators, principals, teachers, school staff, parents, students, and hundreds of nongovernmental organizations supporting the schools were the driving forces making all this possible on the ground. We'd like to thank DoDEA's innovative partnership program for encouraging and supporting university-school-community partnerships to improve public schools and the lives of military children and their families.

Most of all, we want to thank our families who have propelled our lives and this work forward. We want to thank our spouses, children, their spouses, grandchildren, extended families, and friends for their love and encouragement. They are the source of our inspiration.

Finally, we thank everyone for their contributions along this long road. Schools, students, and families are the beneficiaries of your warmth, investments, and use of scientific knowledge to better people's lives.

Introduction: The Case for Monitoring and Mapping of School Violence and Bullying

Parents, educators, and political leaders continue to be appalled at senseless acts of bullying and violence in our children's schools. Incidents such as Columbine and Sandy Hook galvanized the nation and resulted in determined efforts to prevent such acts from occurring. Billions of dollars and endless hours of time from dedicated educators are being invested to help create safe schools for our students.

Much of the effort is driven by extreme acts of violence occurring many miles away and brought home by the media or in response to a rare and dramatic event close to home. Unfortunately, violence prevention efforts are rarely based on reliable and timely information on what is happening in a local school or district.

The lead authors of this guide have been working to reduce school violence for decades. Over these many years, one of the greatest concerns has been that social workers, psychologists, counselors, principals, and parents in local, regional, and statewide contexts don't have reliable or valid local data to ascertain the types of school safety or bullying problems within their school, community, or region.

Educators and policymakers often jump to conclusions about their own schools and student populations and institute policy changes based on something that happened hundreds of miles away and made national headlines. They might institute practices or adopt programs that other schools are using without first gathering and analyzing data on their own schools. This is why it is essential for educators, school administrators, and officials to examine what the data say about their own students.

Each school and community is different. Most parents are aware of this when selecting schools for their children. Real estate prices of homes are often influenced by a school's academic and social reputation. Studies over the past decades provide additional strong evidence showing that schools, even in the same neighborhood and communities, vary widely in the type and frequency of violence and the student subgroups most often victimized. Moreover, schools differ greatly in the resources they have and in their ability to implement programs. Thus, a one-size-fits-all approach to dealing with school safety will likely miss the mark. A gang program may be implemented in a school with no gangs but that instead has high levels of name-calling or school fights. Similarly, a school safety program focusing on sexual harassment may not address the issues in a school with a high number of weapon incidents and threats.

Because awareness of school violence and bullying has grown, over time, schools might have any number of anti-violence, anti-drug, anti-bullying, anti-gang, or positive behavior programs in place to reduce the risk that children will use illegal drugs, hurt others, or ultimately hurt themselves. They may have programs designed to reduce specific types of violence even if other forms of violence are more prevalent in their particular school. This is not a very efficient use of time, money, or social energy when schools have such high demands that go beyond safety issues.

Often, when a violent incident occurs at a school—especially one that captures widespread media attention—principals, parents, pupil personnel, and the general public tend to wonder whether they are doing all they can to prevent a similar tragedy from taking place in their own school.

There is currently a wide array of websites from national, state, local, and non-profit organizations that offer excellent advice, evidence-based programs, and procedures to deal with the prevention and aftermath of violence.[1] In these situations, many educators and support staff will reach out for the latest "evidence-based" program designed to teach students how to resolve conflicts without aggression and calm parents' anxiety over whether what they saw on the news could ever happen at their child's school. Often, states and school districts have a list of approved programs from which to select. Sometimes, schools apply for grants that help them purchase programs to reduce violence. However, we've rarely seen those programs continue once the grant period is complete, and often the community does not know if the intervention worked or not.

From a practice point of view, support staff and educators must be aware of when, where, and in what groups students are being victimized, carrying weapons, distributing drugs, or engaging in other problem behaviors that can limit their futures.

Most school staff members know that there are spots at their school where students expect to be able to get away with things they shouldn't be doing. Monitoring and internal mapping allows them to work with members of the school community—students, staff, and parents—to make those areas more secure and to make better decisions about ways to prevent negative behavior.

By focusing on the locations in their schools or the times in their school day where bullying, fighting, or other behavior problems seem more likely to take place, educators can turn those spots on their campuses into places where all students feel welcome and unafraid.

Systematic monitoring provides a framework to help districts and schools gather relevant local information, process it, and identify important lessons. They use these data to identify practices, policies, and programs that are the best fit for their unique situation, and they follow up to see whether these choices are actually producing the desired outcomes.

Knowing how to use this information in productive, democratic, and supportive ways over time is a key foundational approach to reducing violence and creating safe school environments.

A New Mindset

This guidebook calls for a new mindset that integrates data for each school site over time using ground-up and top-down approaches simultaneously. This new approach toward improving school climate calls for using multiple sources of information to monitor the wide range of issues that students bring with them to school. Educators then design relevant responses to these local needs and follow up to see if changes were achieved and whether new issues emerge, as they often do in this dynamic and ever-changing world.

The authors have worked with schools in Israel, California, and Chile to implement monitoring and mapping systems. Over time, many of these locations have shown reductions in school bullying, school violence, and substance use. Examples in this book will emanate from work in these countries and locations.[2]

In California, the authors worked with eight school districts representing approximately 120,000 students and 145 schools. In Israel, currently all schools are using the monitoring system the authors helped to develop. In Chile, the city of Valparaiso has been using monitoring methods. This work has now been extended to hundreds of schools across Chile. Each of these three sites has reported sustained reductions in school victimization. The most developed and integrated system is in Israel.

The idea of ongoing monitoring of students and schools is not new and is actually comparable to the way educators use formative assessment data to inform academic instruction. In order to monitor the academic progress and needs of students in a school, educators do not rely on national statistics or news stories about other schools. They increasingly conduct frequent and varied types of assessments to track students' academic performance, identify strengths and weaknesses, and design appropriate pedagogical responses. Teachers are "checking for understanding" throughout the week as they prepare students for quizzes, exams, or other forms of assessment. Student scores are the central topic of many teacher planning meetings. Data teams examine which subgroups of students are not reaching the standards. They consider what types of interventions are needed or how to group students in their classrooms to improve outcomes. This day-to-day attention to assessment details in schools is all part of the culture of accountability that schools have grown accustomed to under state and federal education laws.

For many years, however, educators and our nation's political leaders have not given the same level of attention to nonacademic issues in schools. This is changing. The new Every Student Succeeds Act (ESSA), which replaces No Child Left Behind, requires states and schools to have social and emotional programs and measurement systems to help them integrate Social Emotional Learning (SEL[3]) into schools, in addition to the traditional focus on academic outcomes. Monitoring student behavior and well-being with the same regularity with which academic performance is tracked gives school and district leaders a much clearer picture of the issues among their particular group of students.

Monitoring is a social feedback system that continually responds to current and emerging local needs. Monitoring is very similar to the public health concept of "surveillance" used by the Centers for Disease Control and Prevention (CDC).[4] But current surveys, such as the CDC's Youth Risk Behavior Survey[5] (YRBS), provide only a statewide or a national snapshot and are not useful for making decisions about local schools and districts.

Using multiple methods, monitoring allows for flexibility in how feedback is gathered. Whether it's through a paper-and-pencil survey, observations on school grounds, focus groups, or the use of students' smartphone apps, monitoring is about collecting timely information that is more useful than discussing survey results from previous years. School leaders can gather input about a wide range of health and behavior issues or apply strategies that focus on a particular area of concern.

Monitoring creates a culture in which ongoing feedback from students and adults in the building is valued and used to improve the environment in which people learn and work. Educators can find out, for example, who is being threatened, where it is happening, and at what times of day. Monitoring school climate is like taking a school's vital signs and then acting to address areas of weakness and build on existing strengths.

This guide will:

- Shift attention toward considering how adults can make better use of time and space to improve students' social and emotional learning, as well as school climate.
- Describe the components of a comprehensive monitoring system and provide examples of how schools can better monitor risk behaviors, victimization, climate, and student and staff outcomes by listening to the voices of students, parents, and staff.
- Suggest ways to analyze the feedback collected, present it to multiple constituents, and, most importantly, use it to address areas of concern.

Mapping and Monitoring
Bullying and Violence

Creating Awareness and Making a Commitment

The first step toward implementing a monitoring system is creating awareness within the school or district about why, how, and for what purpose the information is being collected and how will it be used to help improve the lives of all school constituents. School leaders can use simple and inspiring examples to learn about the needs of students and staff members and to develop ways to address particular issues in those schools. Leaders may also emphasize the ways a monitoring system can empower students and staff members to make their voices heard and influence a school's direction by bringing attention to their views and needs.

This process, however, will also likely include addressing teachers' and parents' concerns over whether the information collected will reflect negatively on students, staff members, and the community. These concerns are well-founded. Ever since the passage of No Child Left Behind (NCLB), the emphasis on being "data-driven" became a central focus in schools and school districts across the country. But, along with making schools more accountable for the achievement of all of their students also came the side effects of schools being labeled as failures, the creation of a blaming culture, of teachers being suspicious of new evaluation systems that would punish them for students' low achievement, and of parents not being sure what to think of their children's schools (see Box 1.1).

Cheating scandals, school closures, and an inordinate amount of time spent preparing students for standardized tests are some of the ways that accountability systems have affected schools and explain why many educators would be wary of any other attempts to collect information.[1]

While the new Every Student Succeeds Act (ESSA) allowed states much more flexibility in designing their accountability systems, it still maintains a strong focus on monitoring students' success in multiple domains.[2] We suspect that concerns about the effects of accountability may still linger, even with the new legislation.

> **BOX 1.1 Steps to Creating Awareness and Making a Commitment**
> - Explain and provide examples of why monitoring is important for the school.
> - Communicate in multiple ways about why surveys, focus groups, and other methods are important and how they will be used.
> - Acknowledge and address concerns over use of data.
> - Make a commitment.
> - Build a coalition or committee representing the school and community to lead the monitoring process.

Addressing Concerns over Nonacademic Data

While most of the attention in recent years has been on the negative use of academic data from accountability systems, monitoring nonacademic (or what is currently referred to as "noncognitive") data may prove even more sensitive. Naturally, educators have some real concerns about the consequences of collecting and releasing data to the public on negative or risky behavior among students. In fact, the more public a superintendent or principal wants to make the data on his district or school, the more resistance he or she is likely to encounter.

First of all, educators might fear that data showing that students are bringing weapons to school, using drugs, or falling victim to sexual harassment might result in parents pulling their students out of the district and moving them into charter or private schools, or being home-schooled. When schools lose students, they also lose funding—an outcome that often has rippling effects throughout a district.

Others might feel negative toward the idea of monitoring because they think school or district leaders won't do anything with the information they collect anyway. They feel that their voice doesn't matter. Students especially might feel this way if they complained to a teacher or principal about something in the past but believe that nothing was done about it.

Many have already had negative experience with research in general and surveys in particular. They may have already formed an opinion that information from surveys does not translate into something that is useful, something that can guide decisions about students' needs on a daily basis. Based on past bad experiences, some feel that it's easy for school and district leaders to be "drowning" in data to the extent that they don't know which issues or indicators to prioritize. So, instead, the information collected in surveys gets filed away year after year, and leaders don't take advantage of the potential it has to improve school climate.

Educators are also all too accustomed to seeing programs come and go. Many are justifiably cynical toward giving class time to a survey, a focus group, or something else that they view as a temporary solution. But monitoring is not an intervention program. It's creating an environment in which school leaders welcome input—whatever form it may take—and use it to continually plan, implement, reassess, and adjust programs and practices to fit the needs of a school.

It's important for leaders to acknowledge these concerns and build support for a monitoring system in order for it to be useful. They need to explain how this system will be different and how it will be used to improve students' lives and not to punish or label anyone.

Ultimately, being honest about data—both academic and nonacademic—demonstrates that educators are openly recognizing the challenges they face and are trying to address them.

We have learned that sometimes a gradual approach is most useful. A school may start with issues that are less sensitive and less public and ensure that the findings are not presented in public forums. In the first stages of a citywide monitoring system, for example, the findings were presented to city leaders without disclosing the identities of the particular schools, thus shielding the principals from any concerns about repercussions. In later stages of the process, when more trust was established, the schools' identities were shared and the superintendent was able to relate to the particular concerns of each individual school.

Making a Commitment

The main outcome of building awareness is showing a commitment to engage in monitoring. It is best when such a commitment emerges through a democratic process that involves all school constituents reaching a consensus after debating the issues. This is not always possible, however. In some cases, school leaders may face resistance to the process by their own staff members or parents. These leaders may have to make a choice—either postpone the idea and wait for a better opportunity or make an executive decision to go ahead and implement a monitoring system. In other cases, a monitoring system is imposed on a district by the state, or a school is required to adopt a monitoring system because of a district decision or as a requirement for a grant they are receiving.

Research teaches us that even if a decision to implement a program or a monitoring system is imposed by an authority and the school has to follow through, it is essential to continue to build consensus and agreement. Even when a system is imposed, schools can have much to say about how to modify it for their particular circumstances, and raising awareness and building coalitions is always part of the process.

It is important to publicize and celebrate the school's commitment with the whole school community. Even when the decision to engage in adopting a monitoring system has been imposed and was not reached through the gradual process of building a consensus, it is important to embrace it and emphasize its potential contribution to the school and to all members of the school community. Schools may find it helpful to communicate how they are using science and the democratic process of listening to all community members in order to improve the education and well-being of their students. This may also be an opportunity to invite participation and contribution from parents, community members, and organizations to support this important process.

Coalition- and Team-Building

Before any surveys, focus groups, or interviews are conducted, representatives from across the school community—teachers, classified personnel, parents, and, when possible, students—should have a chance to learn about the proposed system and to influence the questions it will address and how the information will be shared.

It is best to have a steering committee to lead the process. An existing group, such as a school improvement committee or an advisory team, could also be doing this work as long as individuals representing all groups are involved. Members of the committee can help determine the topics and issues that will be monitored. They can also help decide which methods to use, how to release the information, and how to plan for ongoing monitoring. It is recommended that the committee includes someone who is a data expert and can advise the others on the strengths and weaknesses of different methods and instruments.

If such a resource person does not exist in the school, it is important to have ongoing expert consultation to ensure that the decisions made by the committee will indeed help the school meet its goals. Universities can be an important resource in this process. Some university researchers may have the interest and skills to support a monitoring system as part of their academic pursuits. In such cases, it is important to first set ground rules and communicate with the researchers on how to use the data, maintain confidentiality, and communicate the results.

This process can also include roundtable discussions with parents, teachers, and others about what they want the monitoring system to include.

Steering committees need to be streamlined to ensure that they can work effectively. In some schools and districts, it may be helpful to have a larger advisory board that will ensure the representation of multiple constituents and voices in the district or school. Such a board could help enhance the legitimacy of the decisions made by the steering committee.

Communicating

Once the committee decides on the features of the monitoring system, it's important to share the information with everyone who will be involved and to provide plenty of advance notice before any surveys are conducted. Schools work hard to make sure students show up on days that standardized tests are given—sometimes even offering incentives and sending repeated reminders home with students. The same strategies can be used to draw attention to an upcoming student survey and gather responses that are as representative as possible.

Schools now have multiple ways to communicate with their teachers, parents, and students, including email, newsletters, social media, school announcements, staff meetings, parent conferences, and student assemblies. All opportunities should be used to present the monitoring system in a positive light and to be open about who will participate, the types of questions that will be asked, and how parents and community members can review the results.

Examples of Monitoring

This guidebook is inspired by 20 years of collaborative work to improve school climate and student well-being. Working with government leaders, district administrators, and school personnel in the United States and abroad, the authors have extensive experience in designing and implementing monitoring systems that fit local needs and in showing how results can be used to improve schools.

These various monitoring models already in use can help education policymakers and administrators gain a better understanding of how these systems can empower schools and guide decisions about programs and interventions.

The overarching message of this guidebook is that methods of monitoring should be well integrated into the process of leading a school, just as academic assessment is. Viewed together, both academic and nonacademic data can provide the information that school leaders need to create safer, more successful schools.

California School Climate, Health, and Learning Survey

The California School Climate, Health, and Learning Survey[1] is a comprehensive set of surveys that includes the:

- California Healthy Kids Survey (CHKS)
- California School Climate Survey for staff (CSS)
- California School Parent Survey (CSPS)

The CHKS is a youth risk and resilience survey given to students in the 5th, 7th, 9th, and 11th grades. The survey gathers feedback from students on issues such as school connectedness, safety, violence and victimization, substance use, and physical and mental health. There is a core survey that covers all of those topics to some extent as well as supplemental modules that ask more detailed questions on specific topics.

The CSSS is for teachers, administrators, and all other school staff (e.g., secretaries, security guards, bus drivers). It asks about multiple aspects of school climate and needs for professional development.

The CSPS focuses on parent perceptions. It asks many questions that parallel those presented to students and staff. In addition, parents describe how they perceive the ways that the school engages and involves them in the school.

For more than 20 years in California, school districts have administered the CHKS but few took full advantage of the information that it provides or shared the results with teachers, students, and parents with the goal of finding solutions or intervention programs that would address problems revealed by the data.

As part of a grant from the Department of Defense Education Activity, the authors worked with the California Department of Education and WestEd, a research organization, to create two military-connected schools survey modules—one for elementary schools and a separate one for middle and high schools. Military modules were also created for the staff and parent surveys. These surveys were integrated into the CHKS, made available throughout California and the nation, and allowed comparisons between the responses of military-connected students and their non-military peers for the first time.

The authors also collaborated with a consortium of eight school districts in the San Diego area, serving large numbers of military-connected students, to make better use of the surveys. As part of two grants, called *Building Capacity in Military-Connected School Districts* and *Welcoming Practices*, educators at the district and school levels learned how to better understand the data, identify the needs among their students, and implement programs or practices to address those needs.

The researchers then worked with the state to insert a military-connected question into the core survey taken by all California students in those grades, demonstrating how existing survey instruments can be adapted to meet specific needs.

Because of the military-connected survey module and the new question added to the core survey, researchers are learning about this population of students in ways that were previously not possible. Numerous academic research articles have since been published and are influencing how schools serve children in military families.[2]

Israel: A Multilevel and Integrated National Monitoring System

The authors have been helping to shape Israel's monitoring system. This system is unique because it integrates monitoring academic achievement with social and academic school climate, and it is implemented on multiple levels. All schools are part of the School Efficiency and Growth Indicators (MEITZAV) system. Students are tested on three to four subjects (English, math, language, science and technology) and respond to an extensive climate questionnaire. Every three years, the National Authority for Research and Evaluation conducts the monitoring system in each school, while during the other two years schools have the option of administering it internally. The results of both the academic achievement and the climate feedback data are provided to each school in the same reports. Schools use this report as part of their school improvement efforts. In addition, some cities develop their own annual surveys for students, teachers, and parents to the climate survey in order to have a comprehensive citywide monitoring system. The reports from all schools are aggregated on the local and national levels to provide a comprehensive view of both academic progress and climate among various groups in Israeli society (e.g., by socioeconomic status of parents and by ethnicity).

Every other year, the National Authority for Research and Evaluation conducts a national monitoring study based on a large-scale representative sample of students and schools (about 25,000 students in 450 schools). The survey instrument provides an extensive and in-depth view of victimization and school climate on the national level.

Additionally, the Ministry of Education Psychological and Counseling Services (SHEFFI) focuses every year on a subset of schools (identified through the MEITZAV) that may need additional help in addressing school climate concerns. These schools participate in an internal and optional monitoring process using a detailed school-level questionnaire intended to assess strengths and weaknesses. The school counselor receives support in using the survey to engage the school in improvement efforts. This information is not shared with others unless the school chooses to involve higher level supervisors.

Several cities in Israel have created citywide monitoring systems. The authors worked with the city of Herzelya to develop a monitoring system that surveys all fourth-through 11th graders in the city, their teachers and parents, and focuses on issues that are of particular relevance to the education system in the city. Reports are provided to each school and school leadership teams meet with the city leadership team to discuss the school-level findings and plan improvement efforts based on the feedback received from all school constituents.

Chile

The school monitoring model developed in Israel, and specifically the citywide model developed in the city of Herzelya, has also been implemented in the city of Valparaiso, Chile, under the leadership of researchers at Pontificia Universidad Católica de Valparaíso and the University of Chile in Santiago.

The USC Bar Ilan research team has also been invited to help create a national system for all low-income schools in Chile, one that would encompass a total of roughly 100,000 students. This system has now been expanded and is disseminated nationwide to all low-income schools in Chile as part of a system to support schools in providing life skills to low-income students.

3

Developing a Monitoring System

The steering committee responsible for developing the system is sometimes charged with creating a system from scratch. In many other cases, they are expected to implement an existing monitoring system imposed by the state, the district, or a funder. Even when an existing monitoring system is implemented, the role of the local steering committee is crucial—there is always a need to make both small and large adjustments and modifications to ensure that the system is most helpful in the circumstances particular to a school or district. Box 3.1 summarizes the key steps for developing a monitoring system.

For instance, school leaders, in cooperation with the steering committee, may decide to add a few questions to an existing survey to learn more about a particular issue of concern to a school. For example, they might want to know how Native American parents view the school's respect for their heritage or if military-connected students feel that their parents are appreciated. The committee may also want to add an additional method, such as a focus group, to enhance its ability to receive feedback on a particular issue.

Funding

Before deciding on the components of a monitoring system, leaders first need to address how to cover the cost. Creating a new monitoring system can be an expensive endeavor, so policymakers should conduct extensive research on what sources of funding they have available before finalizing the components of their monitoring system. Sources of funding might include federal grants, foundation grants, or discretionary funding at the district or local school level. These funds might also cover the cost of having staff people analyze the results and write reports to share with policymakers, parents, educators, and students.

BOX 3.1 Steps to Planning a Monitoring System

Note: It's important not to think of these actions in a specific order. The monitoring process is circular and iterative.

- Decide who will participate in the monitoring.
- Decide what issues/behaviors to monitor.
- Choose the methods to use for monitoring.
- Research funding sources.
- Decide how often each of the monitoring methods should be used.

Making use of or adapting existing instruments is obviously less expensive than having something new created. Partnering with other organizations, universities, or government agencies that might want to have access to similar information is another cost-efficient way to approach the funding aspects of monitoring.

Many monitoring techniques require little or no funding at all. Running a focus group, for example, might only require funds for some refreshments for the participants and pay for the facilitator if a staff member is not available to take on this role as part of his or her job responsibilities. A photo essay on vandalism or graffiti at or around the school could be part of an assignment or extra credit project for students. In addition, administrative data usually are already being collected, but perhaps not being shared on a regular basis with grade-level teams or professional learning communities—the groups that regularly analyze academic data.

Discussions about funding should both precede and accompany the process of developing a monitoring system. While a school team may want to use a certain monitoring method, they may find that the cost is prohibitive. For instance, a phone survey of parents may seem to the steering committee to be a good way of reaching a reasonably large representative sample of parents. This method may prove too expensive given limited school or district resources. The steering committee then may opt for an online survey using free or inexpensive software.

The steering committee will then need to make decisions as to *who* will be included, *what* information will be collected, *how* it will be collected, *when* it will be collected, and *how* often. While we present these questions in a sequence, experience tells us that the planning processes involved are more complex and circular. Sometimes limitations on how the information will be collected can determine the answers to who, what, and when—and vice versa.

The model in Figure 3.1 illustrates the stages of building awareness and mobilizing to create a monitoring system that helps assess the school. As the process continues, the school plans interventions and policies, implements them, and reassesses their

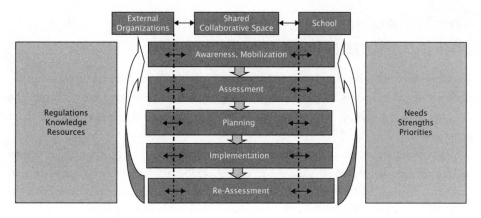

FIGURE 3.1 The stages of building awareness and creating a monitoring system.

effectiveness. The model also shows how a school can collaborate with other organizations, such as universities or community organizations, to create "collaborative spaces" to use external resources and supports.

Who to Monitor

An important question is whose perspective to include in the monitoring system. These various groups include:

- Students
- Teachers
- Other certificated staff (administrators, counselors, social workers, academic coaches, etc.)
- Classified staff (nutrition staff, paraprofessionals, custodial staff)
- Parents

Everyone should have an opportunity to provide feedback on what is happening in the school. Having multiple perspectives provides the best picture of the school. Note that differences between these perspectives are expected, but these differences should not be seen necessarily as indications of inaccuracies, exaggerations coming from one group (such as students), or purposeful underestimates by another group (such as administrators). Different constituents may have different experiences in a school. There are also indications that major discrepancies among the various groups within a school can reflect higher levels of school violence.

If possible, including as many groups as possible is recommended. Nevertheless, monitoring can be quite helpful even if it focuses on some groups and not others. Experience shows that when starting with one group—namely students—gradually more groups ask to participate so that their voices can also be heard.

The Difference Between Sampling and Monitoring Everyone

A survey that uses merely a sample of students, teachers, or parents might be sufficient for some purposes, and sometimes a representative and large sample might be the only option available. But sampling doesn't give everyone the opportunity to share experiences.

Surveys used as part a monitoring system are really a census of an entire school or an entire grade level in which the survey is given because everyone gets a chance to share their voice. This approach should give educators much greater confidence in what students have to say. A survey of all students, staff members, and parents is the richest and most trustworthy source of data.

4

What and How to Monitor

The next area to consider is what aspects of school life to include in the system. In some cases, the topics covered by a monitoring system are predetermined by the state, district, or funder. For instance, schools that have tobacco-prevention grants are required to monitor patterns of student tobacco use. Other times, the school is given at least some flexibility. Schools need to choose what topics to include at what stage of the monitoring process.

There are several issues to consider in making these choices. The most important consideration is the relevance of the topic to current school policies and concerns. Some schools may initiate a monitoring system because they are struggling with major issues, such as drugs or bullying, and they will monitor these issues and the factors that may contribute to the situation. Other schools may be involved in a new program and may want to assess the school's progress in implementing the program and achieving the desired outcomes. The components chosen for the monitoring system should reflect these issues. It is useful to consider covering several major areas in a monitoring system.

Victimization and Perpetration

Questions need to address the multiple types of school violence and bullying behaviors, including verbal-emotional bullying (e.g., humiliating comments), indirect social aggression (e.g., excluding a student), physical bullying, cyberbullying, sexual harassment, and weapon-related behaviors (e.g., bringing a weapon to school, threatening with a weapon). In some settings, it may be important to identify whether students are being victimized by staff and vice versa.

School Climate

This central area includes multiple issues. They include topics such as how students perceive the respect, support, and care they receive from staff; how engaged and connected they feel in school; and whether they are satisfied with their school. Many of these questions are also relevant for staff and parents.

Social and Emotional Learning

Given the importance of social and emotional learning (SEL) and the current emphasis on including SEL in accountability systems, schools may want to consider adding this component to their monitoring. Monitoring SEL competencies may be especially relevant to schools that engage in SEL-promoting interventions.[1]

Safety and Fear

An important aspect of school climate is the degree to which students and staff members feel safe in school. Participants may be asked if they feel safe at school, whether their peers and classmates feel safe, whether the school has a violence problem, and even if they skipped school because they were afraid someone would hurt them. Schools may also present more detailed questions about which times and places in the school are deemed safer or more dangerous. Interestingly, in citywide monitoring, many also ask about fear and safety in the routes to and from school as well as in other places in the city, such as parks and entertainment venues.

Perceptions of School Policies and Practices

Research evidence indicates that students' perceptions of whether school rules are fair and consistent are very important to them. Furthermore, schools that try to implement various practices to prevent violence and enhance positive climate (e.g., active engagement of teachers in the school yard during breaks) may want to gauge whether students notice such improvement efforts. Schools that implement an evidence-based program may want to ask about program implementation to make sure students are getting the dosage necessary to make the program effective.

Exposure to and Engagement in Risk Behaviors

Research indicates that students respond not only when they themselves are victimized but also when they witness their peers engaged in behaviors such as vandalism, substance use on school grounds, and bringing weapons to school. It is important to ask, therefore, about how dangerous the school environment feels even when a participant is not personally involved. Students' engagement in behaviors such as drinking alcohol, smoking tobacco, and abusing other substances are major concerns for many schools. It is important, therefore, to include references to such behaviors to assess how widespread they are. Similarly, many schools try to assess how many of their students have suicidal ideation or even suicide plans.

Attitudes

Schools try to prevent risk behaviors and victimization by trying to impart pro-social attitudes. For instance, schools try to educate students about the dangers of smoking and drinking; thus, it may be important to ask about knowledge, attitudes, and intentions regarding smoking.

Demographics and Background

While most of the attention in surveys focuses on the kind of issues just described, it is very important to also gather basic information about the participants, such as gender, grade level, years working in the school (for staff), education level (for parents), participation in free lunch, ethnicity, and being part of a more vulnerable group (e.g., military-connected, foster care, homeless, LGBTQ, immigrant). These characteristics are important when examining feedback and asking questions about variations among students, teachers, parents, etc. For instance, which groups report the highest/lowest levels of victimization? School engagement? Safety?

By including such questions, the feedback is broken down by meaningful target groups, and educators can differentiate their planning. For instance, females in higher grades might report more sexual harassment than any other group in school, teachers or students who are new to the school might express the highest levels of alienation, or military-connected parents might report not feeling respected by staff.

Districts and schools tend to focus on problems and weaknesses in school life. While these are important issues, including aspects that indicate strength and resiliency is also recommended. For instance, many communities and school are involved in "asset mapping,"[2] intended to identify the resources and strengths of a school and community resources. Learning from the school community about a school's assets and monitoring progress in this area may contribute to school and community policymaking and planning.

How to Monitor

The steering committee must also decide which methods or instruments will be used to capture responses of students, parents, and school staff members. Educators agree that multiple measures are needed to gain an accurate picture of what students know and can do academically. The same approach should be taken toward collecting information on nonacademic indicators.

A survey taken by all students or all students at a specific grade level, for example, might be useful in accurately representing what is taking place in a school, but it won't provide the detail that can be gathered by conducting focus groups with students, parents, or school staff members or by observing student behavior. Here, we discuss several methods that can be part of an overall monitoring system. They are first presented here briefly and then the following sections of the book expand on each of these methods.

- *Surveys* are beneficial because they are able to capture information from a large population of people, such as an entire grade level or even an entire school. Surveys also allow for comparison between schools and over time to see if there has been change on a certain indicator. Decisions regarding surveys include whether to use existing instruments or create homegrown surveys and how to collect valid, reliable data.
- *Focus groups* provide rich detail on a particular topic that can't necessarily be gathered through a survey. Focus groups can be conducted with students, school staff members, parents, and even other members of the community.
- *Interviews* with specific individuals might at times be preferable to gain even more insight and detail on a particular issue. Individual interviews can provide more details on what members of the school community think about why certain behaviors occur in school and how they feel toward staff or the school as whole.
- Structured *observations*, in which the observer(s) are looking for specific activities, behaviors, and interactions, are another source of data that can be used in combination with surveys to work toward continuous improvement in school climate. Observations can focus, for instance, on what is happening in key locations and times in school, such as hallways during recess and locations where students enter and exit the campus.
- With *mapping*, school leaders create an actual diagram that members of the school community will use to identify where and when certain behaviors are taking place and which groups are more susceptible to feeling unsafe in these times and places. Students, teachers, and even parents can use maps of the campus to mark what they have observed or where they have personally been involved in specific incidents. Mapping gives school leaders a much more concrete picture of what is happening inside and outside the walls of the school and therefore can lead to more specific, targeted, and effective solutions to school safety issues.
- *Administrative records and databases* include data on suspensions, office referrals, detention, hotline calls, cases of peer mediation, or other records of students being punished for breaking rules or having conflicts. Other examples would include the honor roll, a "dean's list," and students earning community service hours or points. These databases can be more than just a way to count how many times a student has been sent to the principal's office. They can also be examined for particular patterns and trends over time and used in combination with other sources of information to make improvements.

- *Photos, videos, and other technology.* With cell phones in their hands, students and sometimes adults are now frequently documenting what is taking place in schools and often sharing it immediately on social media or YouTube. While these photos and videos have tended to focus on what is going wrong—bullying, fights, unsafe or unsanitary conditions—this technology can be used in a constructive way to draw attention to a problem so it can be discussed in an honest way or to highlight exemplary events and behaviors. Students can use technology to be part of improving their school, not just using it to shame each other or the adults working there.

Ultimately, the various methods chosen should be used to complement each other and to point educators toward which areas to address. Using multiple methods can also reveal areas where a school is strong and students are thriving.

When and How Often

Finally, the committee planning the monitoring system will address when and how often each method should be used and how to space methods throughout the school year.

A survey that takes up much of a class period won't be used on a weekly or monthly basis, for example, but focus groups with different students can be used more frequently and can provide the type of ongoing feedback that educators need to make improvements in school climate.

It is also important to consider what time of the year would be most effective for data collection. It is likely that surveys on school bullying and victimization would be more useful after the students spent a few weeks in school and are less representative when they are administered in a period that does not reflect the school's regular routines, as when the school year is almost over.

Sometimes, individual interviews, mapping, and focus groups will likely be more useful if used to follow-up on specific trends noted in the results of a broader survey. Other times, these methods may be used in the initial phases of planning, so that such open-ended methods can provide a basic understanding of the issues students, staff members, and parents are facing. This understanding can then be helpful in designing a follow up broad survey of all school constituents. Each school or district has to decide which methods are best suited to its particular needs, when to apply them, and how often those methods will be used.

5

Student Voice

Even those who agree with the idea of creating a monitoring system might still need to be convinced that what students have to say should be considered valuable input in the effort to improve schools, whether it pertains to raising academic performance or to safety, security, and behavior.

Some argue that students are so disinterested in surveys that they answer randomly or give the first answer that comes to mind. Others are concerned that students respond deliberately in ways intended to harm staff members they do not like. Still others are not sure that students really understand the true meaning of the questions and, therefore, that their answers are not usable.

Students, however, are often the best sources of providing detailed information on what is happening in schools and may even provide realistic suggestions on how adults can intervene.

Student Feedback on Teachers and Teaching

Looking at the ways students' perceptions are already being used in schools can help policymakers and educators see how they can be part of improving school climate. This issue, for example, has been debated in recent years as some states and school districts have moved to include students' opinions on their experiences in the classroom as one component of new teacher evaluation systems.

For example, the Tripod survey,[1] developed by Harvard University's Ron Ferguson, asks students how much they agree with statements such as "My teacher explains difficult things clearly" and "Our class stays busy and doesn't waste time." The Tripod was used as part of the Bill and Melinda Gates Foundation's Measures of Effective Teaching project and is being used in districts across the United States, in Canada, and in China.

In a 2013 report,[2] Hanover Research reviewed the literature on using student perception surveys in teacher evaluation and professional development: "Given the consistent findings of the research reviewed for this report, it is reasonable to conclude that student perception surveys can provide accurate measures of teacher effectiveness," they write. "When the proper instrument, or survey, is utilized, student feedback can be more accurate than alternative, more widely-used instruments at predicting achievement gains. In fact, researchers found that the only thing better at predicting a teacher's test-score gains was previous test-score gains."

In their study of eight school districts,[3] Brianna Kennedy of the University of Florida and Amanda Datnow of the University of California San Diego identify reasons why it's important to give students input into reforms that are meant to improve academic outcomes: "Encouraging students to engage in solving the problems addressed by education reform leads students to construct knowledge by solving authentic problems," they write. "The act of involving students in addressing low student achievement may itself lead to advanced critical thinking and increased achievement. Through this process, students also take ownership of the reform effort, increasing their motivation and sense of belonging in the school community."

The same comments can be made in regard to involving students in policies and practices related to behavior, discipline, and school safety—issues that sometimes students have greater knowledge and insight about than adults in the schools.

In the interviews they conducted, Kennedy and Datnow learned of one charter high school where students were repeatedly being suspended for not tucking in their shirts—an issue that could have been used as an opportunity to ask students for their suggestions on how to address the problem or to involve them in surveying students on why they weren't tucking in their shirts.

"Discussions with students regarding such issues could lead to rapid, efficient solutions that reflect broad, inclusive participation of stakeholders," they write.

Kennedy and Datnow have developed a three-tiered model for describing different ways that educators involve students in data-driven decision-making related to reform.

- *Tier 3* is the most common form the researchers found. It involves students in reviewing their own progress, perhaps keeping a data notebook displaying their grades on assignments and tests, and maybe setting achievement goals.
- *Tier 2* is when educators collect data to determine how engaged students are in learning. Methods include evaluating data on how regularly students turn in homework and conducting classroom observations to view students interacting with each other. In some schools, students even participate in these observations. The researchers suggested that schools could push Tier 2 to a higher level by sharing the results on student engagement with the students. "Expanding the exercise in this way would give students an opportunity to reflect on their own affective learning processes, and it would give educators an opportunity to gain insights from students about their own motivations and perceptions of schooling," they write.

- *Tier 1*, the least common but most desirable, involves actually consulting students regarding classroom or school-wide practices and using their input to design or improve those practices. For example, in one charter school system, students evaluated teachers on how quickly they returned homework or whether they adequately explained the relevance of the material they were teaching.

Again, all of these approaches could also be implemented with nonacademic data in mind as long as students' privacy is protected. If something as significant as a teacher's evaluation score can depend in part on what students have to say about the teacher's effectiveness, then it makes sense to also include students in the process of improving their out-of-classroom experiences with peers.

Trusting Student Voices

Using student surveys and other forms of feedback to guide improvements in school climate is a shift toward considering students as part of the solution instead of only contributing to the problem.

In the case of student surveys, some experts as well as practitioners have questioned whether self-reported data from students can be trusted. While there will always be some students who lie, a well-designed monitoring system includes questions that serve as red flags to indicate lying. We list here some specific ways to gather more valid results from students and to guard against false reporting:

- In the California Healthy Kids Survey (CHKS), one of the questions on substance abuse asks students whether they have taken "Derbisol." But Derbisol is not a real substance, and the question is merely included as a way of detecting whether students read the responses carefully and are responding seriously. Other questionnaires use improbable responses as indicators that students are not paying attention or are not taking the survey seriously. For example, if students were asked how many field trips their class took last year, an improbable response would be 10 trips or more.
- Another way to check the validity of students' responses is to insert questions such as "I am reading and responding to this survey carefully," or "My answers to these questions accurately reflect my feelings."
- During data analyses, it is possible to examine whether questions asking about similar issues yield similar results and if the responses are internally consistent.
- Using such methods, researchers have concluded that about 2–4% of students do not provide usable feedback, which is very low and still provides an overwhelming majority of students who are giving an honest report of their experiences.

A true monitoring system asks students the same questions every year or every other year—another reason to have faith in students' responses. If the findings are generally consistent, which they tend to be, that means students would have to have a well-organized lying scheme. Did students in 7th grade across an entire district actually conspire with the students who were in the 7th grade a year earlier to answer in exactly the same way when it was their turn to take the survey? It sounds ridiculous even to pose the question.

Another check for validity of students' responses is how they conform to patterns that are already known to exist. For instance, younger students tend to be subjected to certain types of bullying, while reports of drug use or exposure to weapons are more likely to show up in surveys taken by older students. Violence—whether someone is a perpetrator or a victim—is always more common among boys than girls. Certain patterns also tend to show up among ethnic and socioeconomic groups.

When these patterns hold true, not just across entire schools and districts but also from year to year, there are many reasons to believe that students are responding seriously and providing a valid picture of their schools. When findings are out of sync, change abruptly and extremely, or are very different from established patterns (girls being more violent than boys, for example), suspicion is warranted. So if, for multiple years, 4% of students in one high school have been reporting seeing weapons on campus, and then the rate suddenly drops to 0, that's a good reason to question the data. Results such as these may be an indication that students have been told to not answer the question or not report any weapons. Patterns don't change that easily.

In the example just described, there is a clear need to follow-up with other methods, such as interviews and focus groups, to see whether the school has indeed made tremendous strides regarding reports of weapons. If that's not the case, student reporting on this matter should not be trusted.

The Voices of Staff Members

The voices of staff members are important to any school improvement process. The perceptions of those who work in a school can have a significant impact on the environment within that school. Improving school climate doesn't mean only making sure that students feel safe and welcome and believe that adults care about their academic and social-emotional well-being. It also means that teachers, administrators, and other school staff feel committed to the school, view it as a good place to work, and believe they have a role in promoting positive experiences for all students—even those not in their classes or otherwise assigned to them.

Staff surveys are an important part of a comprehensive monitoring system because they can tell us first-hand about the lives of staff members in school and can also add another perspective on student behaviors. Staff members are an essential source of information on the interrelationships among teachers, administrators, and classified personnel. For teachers and supporting staff members to contribute best to school performance, they need to feel that the organizational climate supports them and their work. Teachers who feel unappreciated and that they operate under difficult working conditions will be less motivated to invest in their work and may burn out faster and leave the school. Such frequent staff turnover has disastrous consequences for students' lives in school (see Box 6.1).

Staff members may feel that asking for students' perceptions of how they teach and run the school puts them in a disadvantageous position in which others can blame them for academic or behavior problems among students. Listening to staff members and their views of the students, the school, and the district leadership is a way of communicating that their opinions and perceptions are valued. It is also a way for leaders to advocate for the importance of listening to feedback and to show that they welcome feedback from staff members about their performance.

BOX 6.1 Feedback on Administrators

Many schools now use the Vanderbilt Assessment of Leadership in Education (VAL-ED)[1] tool to allow teachers to provide ongoing feedback on their principal and other school leaders. The survey instrument covers topics such as curriculum, instruction, professional behavior, "culture of learning," and connections with external partners.

The administrator completes a self-report, and the administrator's supervisor also completes the survey, thus providing three different perspectives. The respondents also cite which pieces of evidence they are using to make their ratings. Results are used to coach administrators on areas where improvement is needed and to inform the training of new principals.

Providing regular opportunities for feedback from staff members is an important way to assess their needs for training and other types of support. Staff members might share their insights and lessons learned about school policies and practices. They can help identify "what works" as well as when policies and programs have unintended negative consequences. Staff members can provide many innovative and promising ideas about how to improve schools and better serve students (see Box 6.2).

Staff members can also provide a valuable perspective on students. Comparing how staff members view students' experiences with how students see these same issues is very valuable—both when the perspectives converge as well as when there are significant discrepancies. Staff members' responses can uncover issues regarding student health, behavior, and well-being that might not show up in the findings of a student survey. On topics where staff members' responses differ substantially from those of students, administrators can follow-up with focus groups, interviews, or additional surveys with more detailed questions in order to gather insight into whether the issue needs attention.

School Example

In one school using the monitoring system, there were major discrepancies in how students and staff members viewed the degree to which staff members humiliate and insult students. Teachers could not understand why so many students complained about something that they thought was happening very rarely. Follow-up interviews and focus groups revealed that only a handful of teachers mistreated students, but that most of the students experienced this behavior from these specific teachers. This finding was then shared with both students and staff members, and the policy implications showed that attention should be paid to improving this behavior among only a few individual teachers.

BOX 6.2 Steps to Including Staff Members' Voices

- Meet with staff to present the whole monitoring system.
- Explain why it's important for them to participate.
- Explain how feedback from staff will be used and how it *will not be used.*
- Discuss how confidentiality and anonymity will be protected.
- Invite staff members to share their ideas and concerns about the system and discuss ways to address them.
- Create a staff steering committee to help develop the content and issues to be covered in the monitoring system.
- Pilot a draft of the method(s) and instrument(s) to be used and receive feedback.
- Revise and implement.
- Analyze and prepare a draft report.
- Present the report to staff members and discuss potential interpretations, lessons learned, and implications for policy and practice.
- Modify, if necessary, the methods and instruments used based on lessons learned.

When staff members are included in a monitoring system, it is also essential to include them in the planning phases for that system. This will increase their support and motivation to participate. More importantly, many staff members can make valuable suggestions on what issues need to be covered and how to appropriately phrase questions in ways to gather the best information. Some teachers are intrigued by the scientific process and become very engaged in the planning and design of their monitoring system.

Finally, there are limitations to including staff perspectives that should be acknowledged and addressed. Many of the issues addressed by a monitoring system could be seen as a way to evaluate staff members' performance. If they are asked to report on violence and safety in their school, they may fear that reporting high levels of violence may reflect badly on them and their responsibility for school discipline. In such cases, they may report an unrealistic or more "rosy" picture of the school than is actually the case. School principals sometimes reported even more positively about their schools than staff members.

This limitation can be addressed in several ways. Treating the feedback from teachers and other staff members with confidentially and using it to initiate school improvement can help to establish a foundation of trust. If the information is used to find "bad apples," or "whistle blowers" or to blame and punish staff members, they won't want to participate.

BOX 6.3 TELL Survey[2]

The Teaching, Empowering, Leading, and Learning (TELL) survey is an initiative of the New Teacher Center (NTC) in Santa Cruz, California. Since 2008, the anonymous survey, which gathers the perspectives of educators about working and teaching conditions, has been used in at least 18 states and several large school districts to ask about issues such as student conduct, demands on staff members' time, professional autonomy, and professional development.

In addition to the core survey, the instrument can be customized to add questions that are important to a specific state or district. NTC houses the responses—a database including results from more than 35,000 schools—and can provide longitudinal and cross-state comparisons. In schools where a minimum response rate has been reached (typically 50%), school-level results are also available.

In Kentucky, for example, the 2015 results showed improvement in those areas that teachers identified in 2013 as being of concern. The results have also been used to address areas of concern for teachers, such as the amount of paperwork they have, class sizes, and whether they have input into decision-making at the school. School improvement plans in the state now include TELL data.

Survey questions shouldn't put respondents on the spot on issues that may reflect badly on them or encourage them to misrepresent reality to defend themselves. For instance, asking staff members whether "teachers in the school are sometimes mistreating students," whether "some teachers are not monitoring student behaviors in the yard," or if "in this school teachers respect parents" allows staff members to think about the whole building while also reflecting on their own practices (see Box 6.3).

The Voices of Parents

Parents are important partners in the educational process. Including their views in the monitoring system has multiple benefits. First, parents who believe that the school is interested in their feedback and takes it seriously become even better partners with educators. They feel important, respected, and helpful and may be more willing to engage in meaningful dialogue with school leaders and staff members. Parents are also an important source of information on their own experiences in the school and on the lives of their children (see Box 7.1).

In one school, for example, parents shared that their child's teachers contacted them only when the child presented difficulties—never when the child did well. Following this feedback, the school changed their policy and made an effort to communicate regularly with parents and to emphasize student gains and achievements—not just problem areas. In another school, military-connected parents expressed a feeling that school staff members did not appreciate their sacrifices and the challenges their children face due to their parents' military service. This input was helpful in developing a school climate that would be more welcoming to military-connected families and students.

Parents can be viewed as the clients of the school. As such, it's important to consider their perceptions of school climate and whether they are satisfied with the services their children are receiving in order to retain these families and attract others. When parents think their children might not be safe in school, they will search for other options. Monitoring parents' perceptions and levels of satisfaction is important in order to make adjustments and to ensure that student families remain loyal allies.

A monitoring system that includes surveys for parents—and other opportunities for them to share their perceptions—can also help educators learn more about students' lives out of school and whether there are any issues that could affect their academic and nonacademic lives in school.

Surveys of parents and guardians, for example, can show whether students have someone at home after school or whether parents feel comfortable contacting teachers if they feel there is a problem.

BOX 7.1 Steps to Including Parent Voices

- Use multiple means to inform parents about their opportunities to provide feedback (assemblies, back-to-school events, email blasts, website).
- Present why it's important for them to participate.
- Invite parent volunteers to serve on the steering committee and help design the entire system (not only the parent part).
- Assure parents that feedback will be taken seriously and will influence school policies and practices.
- Pilot a draft of the method(s) and instrument(s) to be used and receive feedback.
- Revise and implement.
- Analyze results and prepare a draft report.
- Present results to staff members and parent leaders to discuss potential interpretations, lessons learned, and implications for policy and practice.
- Modify, if necessary, the methods and instruments based on lessons learned.

Differences in Perceptions

When children are in the elementary grades, parents typically are more involved in what takes place at school. They might volunteer their time in the classroom, chat with other parents or staff after they drop off or pick up their children, and regularly attend school events or meetings.

But as children advance to middle and high school, parent participation can drop off, in part because they want their children to begin to take more responsibility for themselves at school, but also because children are beginning to distance themselves from their parents and want to be more independent.

So it's not surprising that, on a survey, parents' perceptions of what is taking place in their children's lives in and out of school might be quite different from what students have to say. There can be a variety of reasons that parents' responses might be different from those of students. Students might be well aware that other students on campus are experimenting with drugs or alcohol, but parents haven't heard such reports. A parent might think there is a bullying problem at his or her child's school because the child has complained of being picked on. The student survey for the same school, however, might not indicate that there is any more or less bullying at that school compared to other schools in the district.

By identifying common themes or noticeable differences between students' and parents' responses through anonymous surveys, sensitive topics can be discussed at parent meetings or in community gatherings.

As with staff members, surveys of parents can also reveal areas where parents think they need more support and information. These responses can help administrators plan parent workshops based on parents' real needs instead of bringing in some guest speaker that they think parents might want to hear.

Concerns

Many parents appreciate what schools do for their children and engage in constructive dialogues with teachers and other staff members—even if they have complaints at times. But some schools have difficult and strained relationships with parents. Conversations with the leaders of some of these schools showed their reluctance to involve parents in a monitoring and feedback process that may reveal school difficulties and add "fuel to the fire." These educators were concerned that monitoring would only increase the kind of parental involvement that they don't want.

Leaders in other schools, however, felt that asking parents openly for their feedback is an important means of helping parents feel their input is heard and valued. As a key person in one district put it: "Some of the parents will always complain, regardless of what we will do. This survey will give them an opportunity to vent their feelings in writing. We are strong enough to take their criticism and see how we can improve."

Parents were more likely to share their feedback when they had the opportunity to collaborate with staff members on creating and implementing the monitoring system and discussing results. When parents see that the school is genuinely interested in their feedback and uses the feedback in its improvement efforts, their attitudes may change.

Surveys

Surveys are an effective way to gather large amounts of information from many respondents. They are flexible and can include a number of topics and subtopics that are selected to focus on the unique aspects of a particular school or district. This flexibility means that questionnaires that address multiple issues can be combined into one survey.

There are many good reasons to compose a survey from existing questionnaires and scales. Most existing instruments were developed by experts and tested and improved over the years. Many of them are free, open for anyone to use, and readily available to schools interested in including them in their monitoring systems. Many questionnaires can be found in special compendiums that store large numbers of instruments, often relevant to a particular area (see Box 8.1).

Schools choose from available questionnaires and scales based on multiple criteria, the most important being their relevance to school needs and what school leaders want to know. These decisions pertain to the content of the instrument but also to the language used. Certain wording, for example, is not useful with younger students or might not communicate well with non–English-speaking parents. Some instruments were designed to cover a certain topic in depth, making it relatively long. Schools interested in mixing several instruments to cover many topics may prefer a shorter questionnaire that fits with others in the same survey.

It's also important to give surveys on a regular, consistent basis. Giving a survey only once won't provide school leaders with the information they need to improve school climate over time. A true monitoring system will include administering the survey on an annual or bi-annual basis so that educators can tell whether issues are getting better or worse, which groups of students are affected more than others, and how their schools compare to others in the district or across the state.

Creating a Survey Module

At times, districts and schools may need and want to create their own questionnaires or at least add modules to existing ones. This may happen, for instance, when the school

> ## BOX 8.1 School Climate Resources
> These websites provide resources for school districts working to improve school climate:
> - National School Climate Center http://www.schoolclimate.org/climate/
> - The Centers for Disease Control and Prevention (CDC) also offer assessment tools for measuring bullying, victimization, perpetration, and bystander experiences: (http://www.cdc.gov/violenceprevention/pdf/bullycompendium-a.pdf).

is interested in monitoring the effects of certain practices implemented by the school. To illustrate, schools that may have changed the way that they welcome new students to school or that have introduced a new app to help students report on witnessing or experiencing victimization (a virtual "tip line") may want to see how students and staff perceive the benefits or the negative consequences of these changes.

Developing such an instrument starts best with creating a team that is knowledgeable about the issue and is interested in getting and using the feedback received with the instrument. It is also very useful to include a staff member who is knowledgeable about the methodological and technical issues involved in developing an instrument.

While many of the details of creating an instrument cannot be covered here,[1] the most important step for this team is to "translate" the general and abstract ideas into concrete language and practical terms. This process may be revealing because the team may find that what they thought would be a simple idea ends up being richer and more detailed. Consider a school that is interested in increasing parental involvement in their child's school. If leaders ask parents a straightforward question—such as "How involved are you with your child's school?"—they may get a variety of answers. The problem might be, however, that different parents may have very different ways of understanding the meaning of the term "involved," with each responding to a different aspect or definition of parental involvement.

It is therefore essential to do some preparation to help break down the abstract term into specific areas, such as involvement in helping their child at home, involvement in making decisions in school, initiating communication with the school, or volunteering in school. As more of these issues are discussed and detailed, it becomes easier to ask simple questions, such as whether they help their child with homework, whether they attend parent–teacher conferences, and whether they volunteer in school. Parents will be more likely to answer these more concrete questions in a reliable manner.

Sometimes, a team that has developed an instrument is pleased with how it has turned out and feels that it is a good way of receiving feedback. The test, however, is in piloting and testing the instrument with various audiences so that their reactions are examined and discussed to ensure that the instrument can be used more broadly.

When developing an instrument or adopting an existing one, it is important to consider the following several issues.

Appropriate Language

Careful wording of questions is important in order to get accurate responses from students, parents, and staff members. If the language is too technical and uses education jargon, respondents might be turned off or might not even understand the questions. But oversimplifying the questions can be insulting to those taking the survey.

Piloting the surveys with representatives from different groups and making sure that they understand that they are just testing it out is a necessary step in making sure the questions have the right tone and can be understood by the intended audiences.

Surveys—as well as announcements that a survey will be conducted—should also be available in the multiple languages spoken by parents in the district. During the pilot phase, school leaders will also want to pay attention to whether any of the wording could be easily misunderstood or offensive to a particular cultural group.

Validity and Reliability

Instruments vary in how rigorously they were tested and whether they will produce high-quality information. *Validity* is the extent to which surveys measure what they claim to measure, and *reliability* is how consistent the responses are to the instrument items.

Sometimes, in efforts to make a questionnaire reliable and valid, the developers design a lengthy questionnaire that has strong "psychometric" qualities. But it is hard to include such a questionnaire in a survey that aims to cover many issues. If a survey is too long, students, parents, and staff members might not finish it.

On the other hand, however, efforts to develop short and simple questionnaires can result in an instrument that is not very useful due to the extreme lack of reliability and/or validity. It is important to balance these demands and select instruments that are valid and reliable to a reasonable extent but that are still useful.

Finally, there are many advantages to instruments that are already being used widely. While some popular instruments may not be as good as some of the alternatives, they offer valuable opportunities for comparisons. If a school can borrow a section of a statewide questionnaire, for example, the advantage of being able to compare results with the state or district may offset many of the instrument's limitations.

Some instruments have established *norms*, meaning that certain scores on the instrument indicate that a certain threshold has been reached. For instance, a score might indicate that a student experiences post-traumatic stress. A monitoring system that was developed for a city in Israel after a war included an instrument that allowed for the screening of post-traumatic symptoms among students and staff members.

Closed and Open-Ended Questions

Most questionnaires come with a small set of responses options, such as "yes/no," "rarely," "sometimes," "frequently," and "always." These simple responses are easy to code and analyze. It is helpful, however, to include some open-ended questions in monitoring systems. These questions might read like this:

- What do you think could be done to improve our registration process?
- What can the school principal do to make you feel more respected in school?

Such questions serve at least two important functions. First, they communicate to the persons responding that their individual and unique opinions are valued and that they don't have to feel forced into providing answers that they think are expected. Open-ended questions provide respondents the freedom to express themselves and may provide educators with insights they did not expect and would not have heard if they only used closed questions and prescribed certain answers in advance.

Not only can educators learn a lot from reading the answers to open-ended questions, but including quotations from these responses in reports also helps the audience feel that responses were personal, sincere, and authentic.

Survey Administration Methods

Surveys are administered in multiple ways.

- Pen and paper questionnaires can be completed in a group setting, such as a class or an assembly. Parents and staff members can also complete a questionnaire that was sent to their home. When administering paper questionnaires in person, it's easier to help respondents who might have questions, and, in most cases, it ensures a high rate of responsiveness. Surveys can be conducted during class times. Administering surveys for parents while they are waiting for teacher–parent meetings is another strategy. The downsides are that the surveys have to be printed, staff members are needed to oversee their administration, and the surveys have to be coded for research purposes.
- Staff members and parents can be surveyed over the phone if the surveys aren't too long. When talking to parents over the phone, close- and open-ended questions can be combined, and the responses will provide a wealth of information. Parents are often appreciative of the effort, but it can be quite costly to pay interviewers and

challenging to find a time when parents are available on the phone for at least 20 uninterrupted minutes.

- In recent years, there has been a growing shift toward conducting online surveys using computers and mobile devices. They are easy to create, distribute, and process. In many schools, entire classes of students visit a computer lab to complete the online survey. Students can also complete surveys on classroom computers, tablet computers, and smartphones. Distributing a survey link through an email account is another method for conducting an online survey. When the link is sent to a known list of emails, it is then possible to monitor who is not responding and to send a few reminders (this could be done automatically without compromising the respondents' anonymity). One downside of this method is that as more entities send out links to online surveys, many people feel "survey fatigue" and are not willing to respond to the barrage of requests. It is important to develop the kind of rapport with parents, students, and staff members that would motivate them to participate in (yet another) survey.

Consent

When surveys are part of a required statewide accountability system that also includes academic achievement testing, it is common that the general consent form provided by parents at the beginning of the school year is enough. In other cases, students must agree to participate and have the option of not taking the survey. As to parental consent, requirements vary from state to state and with students' age.

There are two main forms of consent: active and passive. *Active consent* means that parents or guardians must state, usually in a form letter, that they agree with the student participating in the survey. *Passive consent* means that parents and guardians are informed about the survey and are given an opportunity to object. Unless they object, it is assumed that they consent. Sometimes whether active or passive consent is required depends on the child's age. In California, for example, passive consent is required for students in grades 7 through 12 on the California Healthy Kids Survey (CHKS), and active consent is required for students in grades K-6.

For students taking the survey, a written consent form will likely be used. Those taking a online survey would likely click on an "I agree" button after reading a description of the survey.[2]

Anonymity

Most people will be more likely to take a survey and answer truthfully if they are assured that their answers won't be tracked back to them. It's important to make sure students, parents, and staff members know that they will be anonymous and that they should not write their names anywhere on the survey.

BOX 8.2 Steps to Conducting Surveys

- Decide whether to use an existing survey or whether to create one.
- Decide on the administration method.
- Decide on how students/parents will grant consent.
- Decide how often the survey will be conducted.
- Decide on the length of the survey.
- Make sure the survey provides a specific time frame for reporting behavior.
- Make sure the survey specifies where behavior or incidents took place.
- Make sure the survey is not so short that it doesn't provide enough information and not so long that it discourages respondents from completing it.
- Pilot the survey with small groups to make sure they understand the questions. These results are only for deciding whether the wording should be changed, not for drawing any conclusions.

For surveys taken online, steps should be taken to ensure that a person's responses are not linked back to his or her email address. This should be made clear to the potential responders to increase their willingness to participate.

Some survey respondents may want to identify themselves so they receive a personal response. Offering respondents an opportunity to give up their anonymity allows them to receive help if necessary. For instance, in a survey following a stressful war period, respondents (students and staff) were presented with a list of symptoms that they may be experiencing and asked whether they felt they needed help in dealing with their stress. Giving them the option of revealing their identity allowed them to be contacted by mental health services. Box 8.2 lists steps to conducting a survey.

Dealing with Emotional Arousal

Most respondents answer survey questions in a matter-of-fact way. Nevertheless, surveys may have an emotional impact on respondents who have had a bad experience, such as being sexually victimized. Such responses should be anticipated and addressed appropriately. Educators can offer opportunities for assistance to students and staff who may be emotionally aroused or upset due to the survey content. In several surveys, materials containing information on free consultation services that respondents could approach on their own were included. In other opportunities, the school counselor was alerted in advance and suggested to students that if they felt uncomfortable completing the survey, they should approach the counselor who could help them deal with the issues raised by the questions.

Establishing Trust

Respondents will also likely be more comfortable answering the questions if they view the person administering the survey as objective. If possible, it's ideal to get someone from outside the school to proctor the surveys. If teachers are handling the administration, they should give the survey in a class they don't normally teach.

Anyone administering a survey in class should also receive training on how to provide clear instructions to students and on how to create an atmosphere in which the students feel comfortable responding to questions that might be unsettling. Standardizing the methods used across all classrooms in which students are taking the survey will increase the validity of the responses.

Appropriate Length

Surveys that are too long can easily turn off respondents, especially students. But if a survey is too short, school leaders won't get the information they need. The time it takes for a student, parent, or staff member to complete the survey should also be considered during the pilot phase. Students, for example, should be able to take the survey within a class period.

To get data that can be useful to guide school leaders in making decisions, it's important to ask multiple questions on each area of interest, with each question asking for slightly different information.

For example, the CHKS for middle and high school students asks about substance use in four different ways—whether students have ever tried tobacco, alcohol, or drugs; whether they've ever been drunk or high; how often they've used substances within the past 30 days; and how often they've used substances on school grounds within the past 30 days. Additional questions in that section ask students' their opinions on substance use and whether it's easy or difficult for students in their grade to get the substances.

Include Background and Demographic Questions

When survey findings are presented, they often raise questions such as: Is this true for all our students? Are feelings of belongingness stronger among older students? Do families that joined our school recently feel less welcomed than others? Do female staff members feel less respected than males?

Educators should expect such questions and should include items in the survey that allow for such analysis. Some questions may be relevant to most schools, such as gender, age, time in that particular school, parental education level, and racial affiliation. These demographic questions allow educators to look at the data in finer detail by allowing comparison between specific groups. Other schools and districts may want to know additional background information. For some schools, it is relevant to ask about parents' military-connection so that the perceptions of military-connected students and families can be compared with those of the nonmilitary population. When surveying staff members, districts and schools may also want to know the respondents' position (teacher, administrator, support staff, etc.).

In one district, leaders were concerned about differences between homeroom teachers' responses and those of subject-matter teachers. By including this question in the survey, the leaders could see if job satisfaction levels were different and then plan ways to address lower job satisfaction among subject-matter teachers.

Objective Versus Subjective Questions

In asking questions about topics that might be sensitive, it's important to be as specific as possible. Terms such as "violence," "aggression," and even "bullying" tend to be understood differently by different people. So, instead of just asking a student whether he or she was bullied, ask objective questions such as, "Has someone kicked you?" or "Has someone called you a name?"

These types of questions are quite different from more subjective ones, such as "Do you feel your school is safe?" or "Do you feel the adults in the school care about you?"

Both types of questions can provide valuable information, but they should be viewed differently. For example, a highly visible tragedy, such as Sandy Hook, can easily lead both students and adults across the country to feel that their schools are not safe, even if the data on their schools show no upward trend in weapons on school grounds. Media coverage of a violent incident at a school can be a powerful incentive for a principal or school district officials to take a look at their own school safety measures. Without data on specific behaviors in their own schools, however, principals might be left to make assumptions about problem areas.

Include a Time Frame for Incidents and Behaviors

When schools conduct surveys in order to accurately assess students' and staff members' behaviors and violent incidents, it is important to include a time frame in the questions. Without some parameters, someone taking a survey might include behavior or incidents that happened years ago, and the educators examining the data won't know whether the answers are relevant to the school today. That's why, in order to better understand the issues currently taking place in a school, it's helpful to include a time frame with the questions. Adding words such as "last year," "in the past month," or "in the past week" can help school leaders identify which events are taking place more frequently. The shorter the time frame, the more likely the respondents will be to remember the details and provide accurate information.

There are some issues, however, that are still relevant even if they took place over a year ago, such as being threatened with a weapon or a sexual assault. Time frames for these behaviors may be longer than for other behaviors, such as being insulted by a peer.

The School as the Focus

It's also important that the survey questions are clear about the school environment being the focus of survey. If there are questions about having one's property stolen, being punched, or being the subject of mean rumors, those questions should also contain phrases such as "on school grounds," "during school activities," or "on the way to school."

Provide a Range of Responses

Response scales are an important part of collecting specific information. Ideally, survey takers are not only answering whether or not something happened, but also how frequently it is taking place. If a student reports drinking alcohol at school more than three times, that's more significant that if he or she has had a drink once while at school. When asking about victimization, for example, a survey can provide these options: Never, Once, Twice, 3 times, or 4 or more times last month. When asking about a student's well-being, such as whether he or she felt sad or lonely in the past week, a scale could be "seldom," "sometimes," "frequently," or "most of the time." Respondents, however, might not remember specifically how often something has happened, so they might just be offering their best guess.

Focus Groups

A focus group[1] is a meeting between a moderator or two and group of students, staff members, parents, or other stakeholders. In this meeting, the facilitator presents questions or raises certain issues, and the group members share their thoughts and perspectives. A facilitator or an assistant documents the main issues and points raised by the group members.

A focus group is a great way to delve deeper into a specific topic, particularly one that was raised by the results of a survey. For example, if a survey showed an increase over the previous year in students reporting having things stolen, a focus group with students can then explore what types of items are being stolen, where they are being taken from, and any solutions students might suggest.

A focus group could also be one of the first steps in developing a monitoring system. A focus group with parents can help identify issues of concern to parents. Then, based on the information, school leaders may design a survey that asks all the parents in the school how well they think the school is responding to their concerns. See Box 9.1 for tips on how to conduct a focus group.

The participants in a focus group should represent the racial and ethnic makeup of the school, be balanced by gender, and should include those students or adults who are not typically the most outspoken about issues in the school. Diverse viewpoints are important, but it's best not to include those who could potentially argue with each other and dominate the discussion. Be aware of issues of hierarchy and whether some participants are not engaging in the discussion or are not being genuine because of the presence of someone in authority.

Eight to twelve people is usually a good size for a focus group, and about two hours is a good length of time—enough to cover six to ten substantive questions or topics. Less time is probably better if students are participating.

The location in which the focus group is held is important—a conference room or small classroom is probably ideal, but the principal's office, for example, would likely not feel like a neutral setting.

BOX 9.1 Steps to Conducting Focus Groups

- Invite those who are representative of the student, parent, or staff population.
- Choose a neutral location/room.
- Make it a comfortable environment; provide refreshments/
- Choose a moderator who can be viewed as objective.
- Avoid letting someone dominate the conversation.
- A two-hour time period is good, but probably should be less for students.

The moderator/facilitator—the person who will ask the questions—should be someone who is familiar with the school but is not considered part of the administration. Finally, someone should attend the focus group to take notes or record the conversation. If funding allows, a school or a district might want to hire a professional who specializes in focus groups. These people have the ability to moderate a focus group on various topics and will be seen as impartial. These professionals have experience in group interactions and are open and able to change a style of dominance to a more open and less structured one. They can help redirect the conversation if someone tries to take it over, such as a parent activist who has strong ideas about what should be done in school or a senior teacher who is defensive about the ways teachers are responding to violent incidents.

As with most groups, there will be some participants who are more comfortable speaking out than others. A trained facilitator will also work to get responses from everyone involved.

Focus groups obviously are not anonymous, and even if a participant is told that his or her responses "will not leave the room," it's still possible that he or she will give answers that they think the moderator or the others in the room want to hear.

Someone might share sensitive or anecdotal information that they are convinced is based on fact, while someone else might disagree. The participants should be cautioned up front that everyone is sharing their perceptions and that all views are welcome as long as participants don't engage in an extended debate. As with other pieces of the monitoring system, it's important not to view the responses in isolation, but to balance them against other sources of information.

It's also important to share what was learned from the discussion—or from multiple focus groups—so that the participants can know that their input was valued.

Principals often have student advisory groups or "coffee chats" with parents. Instead of trying to squeeze more meetings into already busy schedules, these existing formats can be repurposed to hold focus groups on specific topics and allow a wide variety of students to participate.

Observations

Observations occur in school every day but are often not planned, systematic, or recorded for the purpose of improving school climate. Observations, however, can be a valuable source of information about what students are experiencing in school and where those experiences are taking place, especially when used in combination with other monitoring tools (see Box 10.1 for tips on conducting observations).

For instance, mapping (which will be described in the next section) and focus groups may point out a troubling "hot spot" on the school campus where fights or other problems among students are taking place. Observations of that location can help school leaders understand what is happening in order to plan a solution.

What to Observe

Studies[1] and anecdotal reports have shown that bullying, school violence, or incidents involving drugs are more likely to occur in the common areas of the school campus or in the hidden-away spots that might not get a lot of traffic. Here is a list of areas that may be the subject of an observation when trying to collect information on where problems might take place:

- Common areas, such as cafeterias, hallways. and courtyards
- Playgrounds, the gym (if it's open to students outside of PE), athletic fields, or stadiums
- Routes to and from school
- School buses
- Nearby parks

BOX 10.1 Steps for Conducting Observations

- Decide what to observe.
- Decide how structured the observation should be.
- Decide who should be observing.
- Provide time for discussion and comparison to other forms of data.

Just because students leave campus doesn't mean that adults should no longer be concerned with their behavior. Conflicts that take place in areas off campus often lead to violence, victimization, or other incidents at school.

How to Observe

The observation process should be thought of as a continuum. At one end are unstructured observations in which the observer is looking to take away a general sense of the activity in that area. This less-structured approach provides opportunities to see behaviors that perhaps were not expected—both good and bad.

At the other end of the spectrum are very structured observation schedules that employ detailed procedures and checklists. More structured observations conducted by multiple observers can lead to more agreement on what actually was observed. These are especially useful if the observation is focusing on a particular topic. More structured observations are usually conducted as part of a formal study or evaluation and involve instruments developed for research purposes. Some structure, such as a simple checklist, however, can still be useful in gathering information, especially for those who are not trained researchers.

In observing the playground, for example, the checklist could list negative behaviors such as pushing and shoving, teasing and cursing, or fights, as well as positive actions such as sharing, including others, cooperation, and putting playground toys away without being asked. The observers could mark the gender and grade level of the children demonstrating each behavior. It's also important to note at what time of day the behavior is occurring. These observations could also include notes on whether and how adults respond to what is happening.

If several observers use the same checklist to observe the playground over the course of the week and then revisit the same location periodically over time, they should be reasonably sure of whether certain types of behaviors are increasing, decreasing, or remaining consistent.

It is recommended that observers try not to hide their presence or mislead students about what they are doing. At the same time, observers may want to minimize their involvement in talking with students or participating in their activities (unless they observe a dangerous or unlawful behavior that requires adult intervention). The low profile of observers may help increase the validity of their observations. Sometimes observers are concerned that they may be changing the behaviors they want to monitor. This is a valid concern because most people behave differently when they are observed, especially by authority figures (such as adults in school). Nevertheless, there is ample evidence to suggest that if observers are not talking with students or intervening in their behaviors, students tend to become accustomed to their presence and, after a short period, do not even notice them and return to their natural behavior patterns.

Who Can Observe

School staff members, parents, and even students can be observers if given sufficient instructions before the process. An insider—someone who works at the school—might not be able to observe in an impartial way, but this obstacle can be addressed by assigning them to areas where they don't usually work. An 8th-grade teacher, for example, could observe the playground when 6th-graders have recess.

Outside observers might be objective toward what they are seeing, but they can also cause students and staff members in a school to act differently than they typically would. Past research has shown, however, that it doesn't take long for outsider observers to blend in and no longer be noticed.

Staff members can also go to other schools to observe. Another approach is to involve substitute teachers or student interns. These people are semi-outsiders—they know the school, but they will likely observe with more objectivity than those who are with the students every school day.

Limitations and Interpretations

The behaviors that are most serious and rare, such as weapon use or sexual assaults, are not likely to be picked up by observers. Observations also cannot reveal a student's intent behind his or her actions. That's why observers should not try to interpret what they are seeing. They should only check off what they are actually watching take place. Using the information to determine whether there is a problem comes later as the information is compared to other sources of monitoring data.

During that process of comparison, observers should also be aware that their findings might not match up with other sources of data. For example, observations and suspension rates might indicate a downward trend in certain types of violence. Student surveys and focus groups, however, might still indicate that students feel threatened or unsafe. This could be because there is an increasing awareness of school violence or because students have been encouraged to speak out. Just because one data source seems to contradict another doesn't mean one of them is wrong. Sometimes, the discrepancies provide interesting insights on differences between what is seen by outside observers and what is perceived and felt by those engaged in the behavior.

Examples of Improvements Related to Observations

Observations can lead to solutions that improve the social climate for all students. Here are a couple examples that involved observations of common areas or specific times within the school day:

Pennsylvania

Observations carried out in the cafeterias of several schools in Pennsylvania[2] revealed that students who were receiving free lunch were exposed to public ridicule while waiting in line for lunch. In addition, those who finished their lunch quickly still had to stay in their seats for 20 more minutes—bored, restless, and increasingly disruptive and aggressive. The observations also showed that several of the lunch monitors had simply given up and were no longer intervening to try restore order.

After reviewing the observations, a school safety committee implemented changes that included improving the flow of students into lunch, reducing large numbers of students to a smaller size, and giving them developmentally appropriate activities to stay occupied.

Maryland

In 2000, the staff at James Hubert Blake High School in Silver Spring, Maryland,[3] was considering adding a third lunch period to handle overcrowding in the cafeteria, which at the time was the only place where students in this growing school were allowed to eat their lunch.

Based on her observations, then-principal Carole C. Goodman proposed to the school community the idea of one, 50-minute lunch period. Students would be allowed to eat throughout the school building and could use the additional time they were given to meet with teachers for extra help, work on projects, participate in club activities, or just enjoy the extra time for socializing.

A committee was formed that involved students, parents, and staff members—especially janitorial and cafeteria workers who had strong ideas about the plan. And Goodman communicated frequently with the parent–teacher-student association to get members' input.

After the new single lunch period was implemented, the idea attracted attention largely because of the academic benefits it provided for students. But Goodman, who became an associate superintendent for the Montgomery County Public Schools, says the change also had a significant positive impact on behavior and social interaction between students.

"It took away the tension of cooping kids up in one place while tensions rose," Goodman says.[4] "When a student was upset, there was an easy out and they had access to an adult who could help them. I truly believe it empowered students."

Most of the high schools in the district have since implemented the same approach.

Mapping

Mapping invites school members to be a part of identifying particular problem areas and times in their school. Mapping is another way to collect qualitative data, and the process takes places as part of a special type of focus group. Different groups represent the various members of the school community, such as students, teaching staff, and support staff.

Several variations on the actual mapping process exist. School settings may decide to modify some details of the procedure while keeping the essential aspects in mind.[1]

The Maps

The first step is obtaining a map of the school. The map should contain all internal school areas, including those surrounding the school and playground facilities. A sketch that is used for fire drills is detailed enough. In some communities where students walk or bike to the school—and where there are concerns about their safety—a simple map of the surrounding neighborhood can also be used with participants.

The maps are essential because they focus the discussion on actual places and times and help avoid abstract and emotional discussions. It's important for students and other participants to provide useful information, and the maps help to trigger concrete conversations.

Figure 11.1 is an example of a map that shows where schools are located within a community and the areas around the schools where students are walking to and from school. Note that this, and all other figures in this chapter were originally in color, which helps to emphasize the content of the maps.

Figures 11.2 and 11.3 are additional examples of maps that give students a simple way to identify those areas in the school that they view as safe and inviting and those that they would prefer to avoid. These maps also identify students by grade level so administrators can better understand patterns.

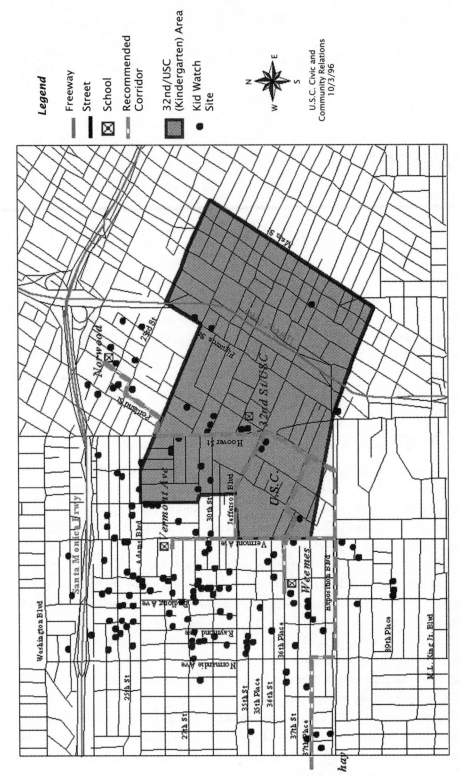

FIGURE 11.1 Schools in a community.

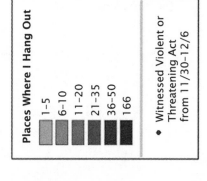

Places Where I Hang Out

1–5
6–10
11–20
21–35
36–50
166

• Witnessed Violent or Threatening Act from 11/30–12/6

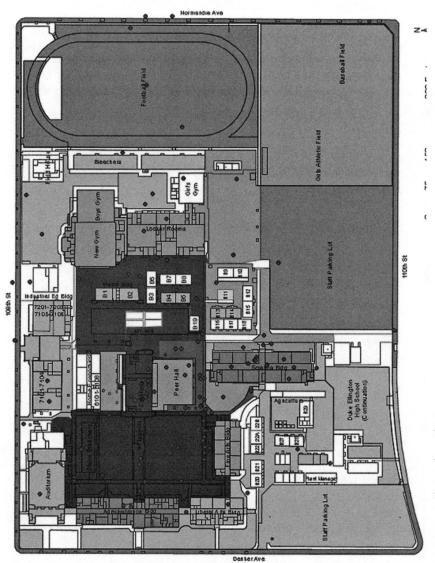

FIGURE 11.2 Places where I hang out.

Campus Map

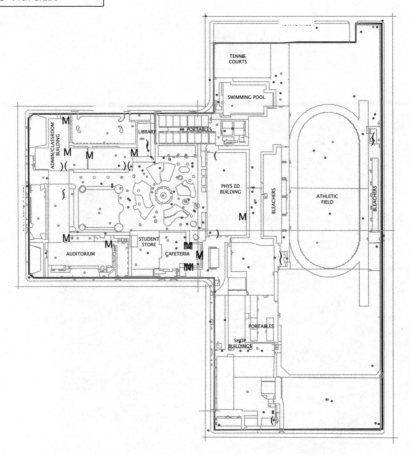

I Avoid These Places
- ● 9th Grade
- ○ 10th Grade
- ● 11th Grade

TENNIS COURTS

SWIMMING POOL

LIBRARY

PORTABLES

ADMIN/CLASSROOM BUILDING

PHYS ED BUILDING

BLEACHERS

ATHLETIC FIELD

BLEACHERS

AUDITORIUM

STUDENT STORE

CAFETERIA

PORTABLES

SHOP BUILDINGS

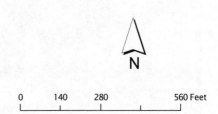

N

0   140   280   560 Feet

FIGURE 11.3 Places to avoid.

Finally, Figure 11.4 is an additional example of a community map that includes schools and other locations where students spend time, such as a park. The streets highlighted are the most common routes that students take to school. When discussing areas in the community outside of school property, school officials can also involve community members and local officials in the process of mapping, reviewing results, and discussing ways to improve students' safety.

The Mapping Process

Focus groups that are using mapping should begin with a facilitator distributing two sets of identical school maps to each individual. Two photocopied maps of the school are needed for each student and staff member (maps A and B). Map A is used to determine what students and staff members believe to be the location of most events involving bullying or other types of victimization (e.g., sexual harassment) in or around the school building. Participants should be asked to identify the locations (on the maps) of up to three of the most violent events that have occurred within the past academic year. Next to each marked event on the map, participants should be asked to write:

- the general time frame of the event (before school, after school, morning period, afternoon period, evening sports event, between classes, etc.)
- the grade and gender of those involved in the violence
- their knowledge of if and how adults in the school responded to the event (student was sent to principal's office, suspended, sent to peer counselor, nothing, etc.)

On Map B, participants circle *areas* or *territories* that they perceive to be unsafe or potentially dangerous. This second map provides information about areas within the school that participants avoid or fear even though they may not possess knowledge of a particular event.

Collecting and Organizing the Data

Administrators can use a table, such as Table 11.1, to communicate the areas within and around the school where students are reporting that violent events are more likely to take place. Organizing it by grade level and gender allows school officials to see which groups of students and areas of the school need more attention.

Detailed responses from students can be organized into a table, such as Table 11.2, to show the different types of victimization they are reporting. The table shows that responses cover areas such as gun violence, sexual assault, and physical fights between students.

School Community Map

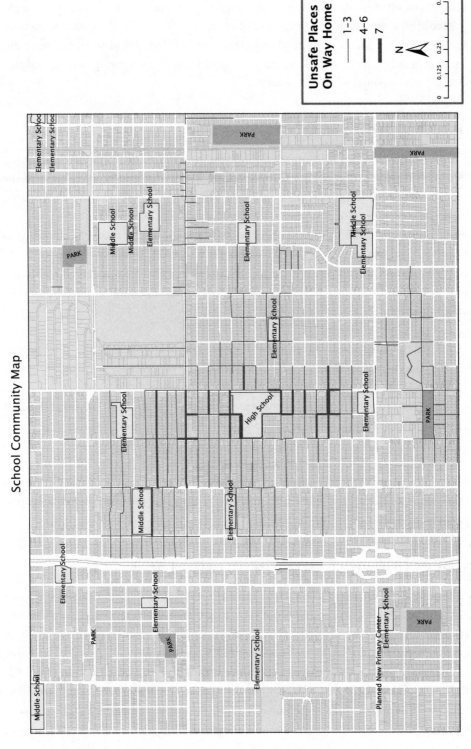

Unsafe Places
On Way Home

—— 1–3
——— 4–6
▬▬ 7

N

0   0.125   0.25   0.5 Miles

Middle School
Elementary School
PARK
Elementary School
PARK
Elementary School
Elementary School
Planned New Primary Center
Elementary School
PARK

Elementary School
Elementary School
Middle School
Middle School
Elementary School
PARK
Elementary School
Elementary School
PARK
Middle School
Elementary School
Elementary School
High School
Elementary School
Elementary School
PARK
PARK

FIGURE 11.4 Routes to and from school.

TABLE 11.1 Location Frequencies of Violent Events by Gender and Grade

Group	Location							
	Class	Hall	Gym	Cafeteria	Outside – on school grounds	Outside – off school grounds	Other	Total
Female								
Grades 9–10	3	21	4	6	1	0	2	37
Grades 11–12	11	21	2	9	4	4	6	57
Total	14	42	6	15	5	4	8	94
Male								
Grades 9–10	2	8	2	7	1	0	3	23
Grades 11–12	1	16	5	9	10	7	1	49
Total	3	24	7	16	11	7	4	72
Total	17	66	13	31	16	11	12	166

Discussing the Results

The group discussion following the map activity should center on the specific bullying events and the areas participants marked as unsafe or dangerous on their personal maps. The overall purpose of the group discussion is to explore why bullying or victimization occurs at those specific times and in those specific spaces.

Use questions such as:

- Are there times when those places you've marked on the maps are less safe?
- Is there a particular group of students that is more likely to get hurt there?
- Why do you think that area has so many incidents involving bullies and victims?

Then, the discussion should focus on gathering information regarding the school's organizational response to the event, the procedures used, whether there was any follow-up, and clarity around the procedures used:

- What happened to the two students after the event, or did the hall monitors intervene when they saw what happened?
- What happens when the students are sent to the office after a fight, or did anyone call the parents of the bully or victim?
- Do the teachers, hall monitors, and/or administrators follow-up on any consequences given to the students, or did anyone check on the welfare of the victim?
- Does it matter who stops the bullying (a volunteer, security guard, teacher, or principal)?

These discussions can show that students and adults in schools often have a different understanding of what should take place when a violent incident erupts—whether they should try to intervene or who they should call.

TABLE 11.2 Students' Accounts of Violent Events

Shooting/Gun	"I've had a boy pull a gun on me in school before."
	"The student that brought in a gun, you know he said, he was saying he was gonna shoot somebody."
	"They were shooting up the school . . . shooting up the door,"
	"My brother got shot in the parking lot."
Stabbing	"We had a terrible fight last year. It was after a basketball game. A couple of people got stabbed . . . It was bad."
Rape/Sexual assault and harassment	"This girl, she got raped by this boy . . .."
	"I seen plenty of guys down there calling females from the end of the hallway . . .. Calling females, like come here, you know. They won't rape you, but they'll harass you to have sex with them."
	"I've told plenty of times of guys messing with me, and you know they say 'I'll talk to him.' I mean talking ain't going to do nothing cause they gonna keep doing it."
Physical fights/ assaults	"Well, I saw a fight. You know, I went up to the second floor. Two girls was fighting and pulling on each other's hair and calling each other names and stuff. That was real violent."
	"Some girls rode up in a car and jumped out and had like these little sticks or bats or whatever you call them . . . and they jumped these two girls."
	"One looked away and some dude just sucker punched me. I went out, like I slammed my head on the concrete. I got knocked out."
	"Before a school dance a group of guys—not from our school—jumped some kids coming in. They broke bottles, and there was physical fighting and a threat of a gun."
	"Members of two gangs got in a scuffle around lunch time."
	"I saw two guys jump one guy. His face had indents where the knuckles had hit." "A boy from our school tried to run over a person from another school."

The facilitator should also explore participants' ideas for solutions to the specific bullying problems with questions such as:

- Can you think of ways to avoid bullying or victimization in that place?
- If you were the principal, what would you do to make that place safer?

In addition, facilitators should probe participants to identify any obstacles they foresee with implementation of these ideas:

- Do you think that type of plan is realistic?
- Has that been tried before? What happened?
- Do you think that plan would work?

Such obstacles could range from issues related to roles (e.g., "It's not my job to monitor students during lunch"), to discipline policies and issues of personal safety (e.g., "I don't want to intervene because I may get hurt").

In schools that already have programs designed to address school violence, specific questions should be asked about whether these programs are actually being implemented and about the effectiveness of those interventions, why they work or do not work, and what could be done to make the current measures more effective.

Adding It Up

Transferring all of the reported events onto one large map of the school enables participants to locate specific "hot spots" for violence and dangerous time periods within each individual school. The combined data are presented to all school constituents, and they are asked to once again discuss and interpret the maps.

Staff members and students use the maps and interviews to suggest ways to improve the settings. For example, in one high school, dangerous incidents were clustered by time, age, gender, and location. In the case of older students (grades 11 and 12), events were clustered in the parking lot outside of a gym immediately after school, whereas for younger students (grades 9 and 10), incidents were reported in the lunchroom and hallways during transition periods.

For this school, the map suggested that interventions be geared specifically toward older students, directly after school, by the main entrance, and in the school parking lot. Students and teachers agreed that increasing the visible presence of school staff members in and around the parking lot for 20 minutes after school had great potential for reducing many violent events. Younger students were experiencing violence mainly before, during, and after lunch, near the cafeteria. Many students expressed feelings of being unsafe between classes in the hallways.

As noted, mapping can show that students, teachers, and administrators may have differing viewpoints regarding the organizational response of the school when victimization happens. Communicating the diversity of responses to students, staff members, and administrators can provide an opportunity for reflection and may generate ways to remedy the bullying or victimization problem in certain situations. When the data are presented to students, teachers, and administrators, they can center their discussions on why those areas are dangerous and what kinds of interventions could make the location safer.

School Example: Cool and Hot

One variation of the mapping technique, for example, has been used as part of a youth dating violence prevention program in New York City middle schools.[2] As part of the curriculum, students learned about personal boundaries. Then they mapped those areas of their school that they considered to be "cool," or comfortable and safe, and "hot," meaning uncomfortable, unwelcoming, and unsafe.

As part of the mapping process, students were asked to consider what they perceived to be "cool" or "hot" locations in the school. Their answers might depend on their age, gender, and even their physical size—and this is important for adults to recognize. Adults reviewing the students' maps were asked to consider questions such as: Is there more surveillance or a greater adult presence in "cool" areas, and do older students congregate in areas that younger students deem "hot?"

Adults also presented the results of the mapping process to the entire school and discussed the next steps they might be taking to improve students' sense of safety and comfort at school.

The researchers who designed the program, led by Dr. Bruce Taylor at the University of Chicago, stressed in their final report that the mapping process can be implemented with very little cost to schools, yet it was popular with teachers. Gathering support from the staff is important in order for students to be given the opportunity to participate in mapping during the school day.

In other schools, the mapping process has led to a variety of solutions that improved daily experiences for students in school. These responses have included adding more adult supervision during certain times of the day, relocating bus stops so students don't have to wait in areas that they feel are unsafe, and closing certain areas of the campus at certain times or opening other areas so students have additional options for where they can eat or study during breaks.

It's also important to note that if one solution doesn't seem to work—meaning that if conflicts or similar incidents continue to happen—that doesn't mean that mapping didn't work. Mapping is not a pre- and post-test method. It is part of an ongoing monitoring process that can lead to a variety of solutions that improve students' and adults' sense of safety and well-being.

12

Administrative Records

Schools maintain a variety of records, but these aren't necessarily analyzed as a source of data for improving school climate. Records of office referrals, suspensions, peer mediation cases, students serving detention, and other incident reports can be examined to learn about disciplinary issues and the school's response. In addition to getting a sense of how many disciplinary infractions take place in school, it is also valuable to detect changes over time. By examining suspension records over a period of years, school leaders may realize that, along with their efforts to improve school climate and prevent violence, there is also a major increase in suspension rates, an indication that perhaps administrators have used suspension as a major strategy. Given the evidence on the negative outcomes of repeated suspensions, school leaders might reconsider their approach to violence prevention or punishment.

Other schools may find that suspensions actually went down when climate improved because fewer students were being disciplined for incidents of violence.

While many schools maintain paper records that are difficult to examine and process, others have computerized their reporting system. When computerized databases are available, the potential for educators to learn from the information and make improvements increases dramatically. Careful analysis of existing records can help identify what grade levels of students are most involved in certain behaviors and whether certain students or groups are committing the bulk of infractions.

Analyses of these records can also help administrators to understand more about why students are getting in trouble, which students seem to be repeat offenders, and perhaps where and when the incidents are taking place. Absenteeism rates should also be examined in combination with other indicators. Patterns in the data can then be used to see what type of changes might be needed to eliminate the reasons that the students are getting in trouble.

These records can also show whether there are certain times during the school year when problems are more likely to occur, such as at the beginning of the year or just before a break.

Records of positive behavior are also kept in databases. These would include the honor roll or a dean's list and students completing community service or participating in volunteer projects. Other sources of information could include students who attend after-school programs, those playing on sports teams, and those who transferred into the school during the year.

The use of administrative records should be done with caution. Certain events are not recorded systematically or in similar ways by personnel from year to year, meaning that observed changes over time may reflect differences in record keeping more than actual changes in behavior. Comparisons across schools can also be difficult due to different documentation styles; one school may record every infraction, even the small ones, while others tend to record only major serious incidents.

With appropriate planning, however, these databases can inform local schools' efforts to improve school climate and provide additional support where students need it. Office referrals should be well documented, provide clear information on the reason for the referral, and identify the characteristics of the students involved, such as their grade and gender. Administrators should also keep information on how staff members responded to the issue. Computerizing these records is essential in order to use them productively.

Examples of Tools

- The School-Wide Information System (SWIS),[1] developed by the University of Oregon faculty in partnership with school personnel, is a web-based software system for collecting and summarizing office discipline referrals in schools. The system was designed to be used as part of the Positive Behavior Interventions and Supports system in schools. SWIS provides schools with accurate, efficient, and practical information to make decisions about school-wide discipline policies. In fact, research shows that schools adopting the SWIS standardized office referral form, clear definitions of behavior violations, and clear process for computer entry and analysis obtain more valid discipline data than typical incident reports.[2] Examples of the tables that administrators and district leaders can generate with SWIS are shown in Figures 12.1 and 12.2.
- A related example comes from the Cincinnati Public Schools, which worked with Microsoft, Proctor & Gamble, and the Strive Partnership to create the Learning Partner Dashboard.[3] Because so many of the district's students are receiving services and involved in enrichment programs provided by outside partner organizations, the website was created to allow schools and those partners to communicate with each other about students' needs. Each night academic and nonacademic data are updated in the system, which allows schools and providers to see who is receiving what services. The program led, for example, to after-school providers holding slots open for students most in need of tutoring or enrichment support instead of letting families sign up on a first-come, first-served basis.

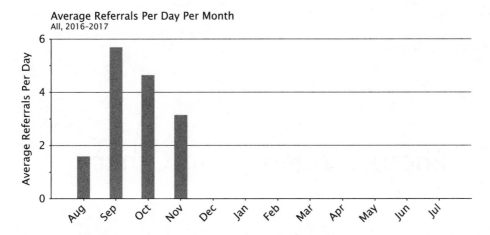

FIGURE 12.1 Average referrals per day per month. Copyright 2016 Educational and Community Supports, University of Oregon. Reprinted with permission from author.

An anecdotal example from the *Building Capacity* districts shows how office referral data can inform which students to choose for a particular intervention. In 2012, San Onofre School began implementing Learning Together,[4] a peer-tutoring program in which students tutor those who are two grade levels below them, such as 5th and 3rd or 8th and 6th. But instead of being the top achievers in their class, the tutors are performing below proficiency and sometimes have behavior issues in class. An assistant principal reported[5] looking at administrative records to identify those who were "frequent flyers" to the office when deciding who might benefit most from the program.

Being a tutor gave the students leadership opportunities that they might not have been offered otherwise. A later evaluation showed that many tutors felt they became more respectful toward their teachers and that they were able to help the younger students learn new things. Scores in math—the focus of the tutoring program—also increased among both the older and the younger students.

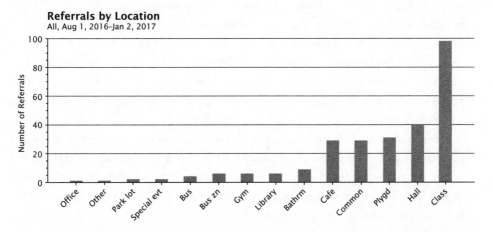

FIGURE 12.2 Referrals by location. Copyright 2016 Educational and Community Supports, University of Oregon. Reprinted with permission from author.

Photos, Videos, and Other Technology

On their own, photos and videos are not a reliable source of information about what is taking place in a school. It's easy to react emotionally or with outrage to a video of a fight, a child being picked on, or some other display of abuse or wrongdoing. But everyone knows from highly publicized incidents posted on YouTube, Twitter, or other social media sites that photos and videos can be taken out of context.

They tell a story, but they don't tell the whole story. Even so, they can be used by administrators to discern whether the action shown in the photo or video is an isolated incident or could be a symptom of a larger problem.

If an alarming photo or video taken at a school is receiving attention from the media, it's better to talk about it with the school community as soon as possible than to pretend it didn't happen. Situations like these create an opportunity to examine and share other sources of data about school safety, violence, and victimization. Too often, one incident can cause the public to draw conclusions about a school that are not accurate. That's why a monitoring system is necessary—to put such an incident in context. Administrators who can refer to other sources of data regarding violence, drug use, or weapons can respond with more confidence when faced with criticism over one incident.

As part of a monitoring system, photos, videos and other technology can be used for positive purposes. They allow students who might skip questions on a survey or don't want to speak up during a focus group to express themselves in a different way.

There are many examples of projects in which students are given cameras and microphones and encouraged to express themselves and present their experiences in school through this media. In addition to the individual students benefitting from such experiences, school leaders, staff members, and parents get the opportunity to see the school from the students' perspectives.

Students involved in such projects, however, should first receive training on when it is and isn't OK to video or photograph people in school and what can and cannot be posted on the internet. The students and their parents might have signed a form outlining appropriate cell phone use at the beginning of the year, but it's likely that the students will need more explanation.

Social Media

Students are always discovering new apps to communicate with each other. While posts on social media might not be considered data as part of a monitoring system, it is certainly the way that children and teens are expressing themselves. Like photos, tweets and posts can be taken out of context and are not reliable sources of information on their own. But posts and comment threads can point administrators to students who might need help or alert them to potential problems. In combination with other sources of information, students' tweets and posts can be a window into what students are experiencing at school, as well as other issues that could affect their lives in school.

While some school districts have been known to contract with technology firms to monitor students' posts, Justin W. Patchin, co-director of the Cyberbullying Research Center writes that schools do have some responsibility to monitor students' posts[1]: "I don't feel, however, that schools should need to go on fishing expeditions where they scour the Web and social media for inappropriate behaviors," he writes. "I feel that schools should work to develop a culture where everyone looks out for everyone else and if something of concern arises, someone will step up and take appropriate action. Most of the time, when there is a threat to cause harm—either to one's self or others—someone sees or hears about it. What do they do at that moment? Are they empowered to take action themselves? Do students feel comfortable talking with an adult at school about what they witnessed or heard about? Do they feel that telling an adult at school or at home would resolve the situation?"

Ultimately, Patchin writes, the goal is for students to feel comfortable about coming forward with concerns and to be "on the lookout for trouble" since they might be reading posts by students who don't have public accounts.

Social media posts have certainly been used to embarrass, threaten, and intimidate other students, but they can also be used by students to raise awareness of certain issues, start a conversation, or get others involved in positive activities. Students can create a hashtag on Twitter or tell a video story on Snapchat.[2]

The following sections describe examples of ways that students are interacting with technology to raise awareness of an issue and provide feedback on school life.

Facebook

School or classroom Facebook pages can be used to gather feedback from students on school assignments, but also on any nonacademic issues that arise among students or on campus. If the mapping activity, for example, reveals conflicts between students in the hallways, students can offer suggestions on how to prevent problems or ideas for how to welcome new students. Moderated by an adult, the discussions can be a useful way to get student input on a wide range of topics. Facebook provides guidance[3] on how educators can use the platform.

Another advantage of using Facebook in the classroom is that it gives educators an opportunity to teach students about the proper use of social media, how to protect themselves online, and how to communicate appropriately. The Pasco County Schools in Florida even created a video[4] that describes how schools are using Facebook to improve engagement with both students and parents (Figure 13.1).

Example: Mapping with Photography

When the San Diego-based AjA Project[5] put cameras into the hands of urban middle school students and asked them to capture photos related to the topic of bullying, they found that the students could express thoughts and ideas that they might not have shared otherwise. The project, called PhotoCity, ran as a semester-long after-school program at Monroe Clark Middle School in San Diego. PhotoCity uses photography and the visual arts as a platform to engage young people in improving their communities.

Click here to learn how to create your own Facebook page

▶ ▶❙ ◀)) 0:21 / 4:39   ⚙ ▭ ⌗

FIGURE 13.1 The Pasco County (Fla.) schools created a video on how to use Facebook to improve student and parent engagement.

"Their images become a starting point for discussions with local stakeholders; with young people taking the lead on intervention and community development strategies needed to promote change," says Melinda Chiment, the AjA Project's executive director. The arts, she adds, give young people "an opportunity to tell their story, and the stories of their community, in a safe and inspiring space."

Using photography as a participatory research tool put some control back into the hands of students who might have felt victimized at school but never told anyone about it. The students were given instruction on how to use the cameras and apply creative lighting techniques. They photographed places where they had been bullied or places where they felt scared to walk, as well as places where they felt happy or thought were pretty. Figures 13.2 and 13.3 show samples of the photos captured by students during the project.

The program also included a lot of reflection and discussion. The students talked about different forms of bullying—such as subtle insults that students might just come to accept. They were also asked to explore what they might have done to bully someone else.

Taking the photographs and participating in the class would not have had much meaning for the students if no one listened to what they had to say. They wanted local law enforcement to know what they had to say. Fortunately, they had a supportive principal who showcased their work in the school and organized an anti-bullying week for students. The PhotoCity students also spoke at a community forum on their experiences.

Photovoice

Developed by Caroline Wang of the University of Michigan and Mary Ann Burris of the Ford Foundation, Photovoice[6] is described as an action research method in which

FIGURE 13.2 A shot of lunch tables taken during the PhotoCity project. Credit: AjA PhotoCity Participant.

FIGURE 13.3 School steps, shot by a student in PhotoCity. Credit: AjA PhotoCity Participant.

individuals take photos to express what they see as the strengths and weaknesses in their communities. The process is intended to give a voice to those who are not usually represented in decision-making or who feel that those in leadership positions are not listening to them.

In schools, this could mean involving students in a project to photograph areas of their campus or neighborhood that are troubling in some way, as well as areas that bring positive feelings. Photos are examined and discussed for the purpose of making improvements.

Unlike students just snapping photos with their cell phones and posting them to social media, Photovoice involves advance learning about taking photos, obtaining the permission of anyone shown in the photo, and thinking critically about what the participants want their photos to communicate.

Photovoice, for example, was used with a group of adolescents who attended a teen center in Baltimore.[7] The program involved a series of 20 sessions in which the students took their photos, discussed them, and learned how to write captions. Exhibits featuring the photos were also held in the teen center, a university, and other community locations. In an article about the project that appeared in *Health Promotion Practice*, the authors wrote about how a photo of a crumbling classroom ceiling, taken by a 12-year-old, caught the attention of someone from the state comptroller's office.

Student Blogging

Student and classroom blogs are one strategy that teachers are increasingly using to build technology literacy in their students and to keep them engaged in the content being taught. Pernille Ripp, a 5th-grade teacher at West Middleton Elementary School

BOX 13.1 Using Twitter in Positive Ways with Students

"30 Innovative Ways to Use Twitter in the Classroom"[9] by Pamela Loatch appeared on the Edudemic website and provides multiple suggestions for ways that educators can use Twitter with students. These suggestions include:

- Having a designated students tweet what they learned that day.
- Sending reminder tweets about homework, tests, or project due dates.
- Documenting a field trip with Twitter, using tweets, photos and videos.

in Verona, Wisconsin,[8] also uses a classroom blog to let her students express themselves about what is happening in class, in their school, and in the world. Instead of it being used as a forum to say hurtful things about each other—cyberbullying—the blog has actually created a sense of community, Ripp says, because she works hard in advance to create expectations for how the blog would be used.

"My students really open up their hearts about things on our blog," she says. "It has been an incredible tool to start discussions about their lives and how they view their role as students. It can really build trust between a group of kids and their teachers."

Discussion threads have included comments on a new internet filter at the school that was making it difficult for students and teachers to get to the websites they needed for assignments and lesson planning, as well as requests (from students) for longer recess periods and their suggestions for an ideal class. While Ripp moderates the students' posts, she does not dictate what they write.

Box 13.1 describes another method that uses social media to connect teachers with students.

14

Analysis and Presentation

When school leaders begin collecting more data and feedback from multiple groups or receive the results of statewide surveys, the information might at first create more confusion than clarity about the needs within a school. It is important to have an organized way of looking at the data, either by asking for specific answers from those providing the data or by developing a plan to analyze the collected data. The questions can be organized under several rubrics.

What Is the Situation?

Feedback can be used to assess how the school is doing on a range of issues, as mentioned in earlier chapters. These include questions such as: How many students reported being victimized last month? What were the types of victimization? What do students think about their social-emotional skills, such as their ability to deal with interpersonal conflict? How satisfied are parents with teachers' performance? How safe do teachers feel?

Is the Situation Different for Different Groups and Settings?

Are there differences in the victimization of students in different grade levels? Are female students vulnerable to certain types of victimization more than males? Do first-generation students feel welcomed in schools more or less than do second-generation immigrant students? Do teachers in the district feel safer than administrators? Do military-connected parents feel less respected than other parents? Are hallways safer than playgrounds or other outside areas?

Has the Situation Changed Over Time?

Are there fewer weapon-related incidents than in previous years? Do students engage in risk behaviors less than in the past? Do teachers think that students have better social-emotional skills? Do staff members feel more supported by school leaders than they did in the last survey? Are parents engaged in school activities more than they were last year?

Did the Situation Change More or Less for Different Groups and Settings?

Sometimes educators are concerned that although positive changes did take place in school, they may have not been uniform, and some groups did not make the same progress as others. For instance, although overall there are fewer incidences of substance use in school, changes may have been less evident among gang-affiliated students.

Other comparisons can be made between groups that received certain interventions or participated in a school safety program and those that did not. For school districts that have introduced several programs, relevant questions pertain to differences in outcomes between these programs:

- Do students who have participated in an anti-bullying program engage in more empathetic behaviors toward victimized students than do students who were not part of the program?
- Is it true that students who received training in social-emotional skills are less involved in perpetrating violence?

How Do Schools Compare with Others?

Sometimes, in order to get a perspective on the situation of a particular school, it is helpful to compare with others. When a school finds out that a quarter of its students complain that a teacher humiliated them, it is helpful to know whether in a neighboring school the figure is 5%, 25% or 50%. Although school administration may find the figure unacceptable regardless of how others are responding, still, the comparison may be helpful in prioritizing the issue. A school that has not made progress in reducing the number of gang-affiliated students may find it useful to learn that most other schools in the district report that their numbers have actually risen significantly.

Sometimes the picture received from multiple sources, methods, and over time is quite complex and confusing. But just because one data source seems to contradict another doesn't mean one is wrong. It simply means that the story is more complex than first realized.

For example, it won't always be clear which students are victims and which students are victimizing others. It's not unusual for a student to be in both positions, and this is an area where data can help inform educators of the behavior patterns in their school. A mix of quantitative and qualitative methods gives school leaders and student support personnel a better grasp on which students are harming others, which students are being harmed, and when this behavior is more likely to take place.

Ways to Present the Monitoring Feedback

Feedback is gathered in order to plan and make decisions about improving school climate. As such, it is important to present it to all relevant audiences in ways that will help them use it effectively. Data should be presented in a way that is sensitive to the specific audience. While some teachers and parents may be comfortable making sense of charts and graphs, many others may find numbers intimidating and unhelpful.

Sometimes it may be enough to summarize the complex picture in a few short sentences, such as: "Fifty percent of our students complain that they were victimized last month, with the most common report being verbal abuse," "thirty-five percent report such an incident," or "forty percent of our female teachers say they feel unsafe in the school parking lot, while only five percent of our male teachers make such report." Other times it may be helpful to provide a richer presentation, covering a wide range of findings. In this case, a table, such as Table 14.1, might be useful.

The advantage of such a table is that it helps present a large set of numbers. This does not mean that readers need to examine each and every number in this table. By sorting the table according to the frequency of the type of victimization, for example, the readers' attention can be drawn to the top (most frequent types of victimization) and

TABLE 14.1 Frequency of student victimization in the past month

	Never		Once-twice		More	
	N	%	N	%	N	%
A student seized and shoved you on purpose	383	51.1	270	36.0	97	12.9
You were involved in a fist fight	509	67.9	173	23.1	68	9.0
You were kicked or punched by a student that wanted to hurt you	513	68.4	173	23.0	65	8.6
A student used a rock or another instrument in order to hurt you	564	75.2	148	19.7	38	5.1
Another student took your things away from you by force	604	80.5	114	15.2	32	4.3
You were involved in a fight, hurt and required medical attention	665	88.7	21	2.8	64	8.5
A student gave you a serious beating	674	89.8	25	3.3	52	6.9
A student cut you with a knife or a sharp instrument on purpose	707	94.3	11	1.4	32	4.3

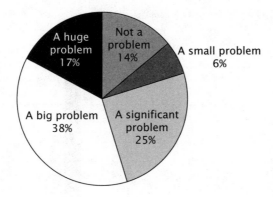

FIGURE 14.1 An example of a pie chart.

to the bottom (least frequent) totals. A few sentences added to the table can help orient the reader as to what is outstanding in the table.

Another way to present data is through charts. The following sections describe several common types of figures that schools and districts may want to consider in presenting the feedback received through a monitoring system.

Pie Charts

The pie chart in Figure 14.1 is used to present the distribution of a single item, showing the relative frequency of each of its categories. The relative magnitude of each of the chart segments is presented vividly, and the person viewing it can see at a glance which situations occur more or less frequently.

Bar Graphs

Similar to a pie chart, the bar graph shown in Figure 14.2, can present the frequency of each category in a survey question. It is also useful when one wants to compare the distribution between two or more groups, such as between boys and girls.

A bar graph is also very useful for presenting the distribution of a number of items to help the reader see how these items differ. For instance, it is easy to see in Figure 14.3 that certain victimization types are much less prevalent than others. It is also interesting to note that in the least prevalent and more serious types of victimization (such as being cut with a knife and receiving a serious beating), students tend to report that it happened to them more than once or twice. This may indicate that a small fraction of the student body is being victimized frequently, while almost all other students are not at all victimized.

Time Trend Charts

A time trend chart, as shown in Figure 14.4, is recommended for representing whether there is evidence that things have changed and whether the change is uniform across groups.

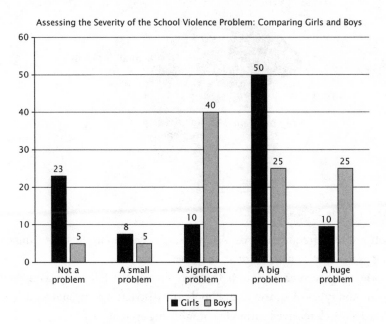

FIGURE 14.2 An example of a bar graph.

The graph in Figure 14.4 shows very clearly that while there is significant reduction in involvement in physical fights among white students, there is an increase among Latino/Latina students and that no clear trend exists among African-American students.

Staff Expertise

Even if district leaders believe that data should be widely disseminated, another obstacle they might face is not having a staff person[1,2] who is equipped to find the school's story by reviewing the data, digesting what the results have to say, and then presenting it in an

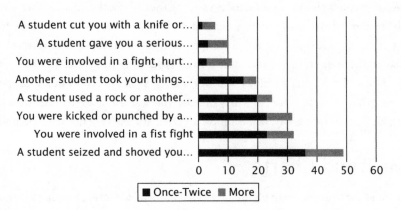

FIGURE 14.3 Another bar graph example.

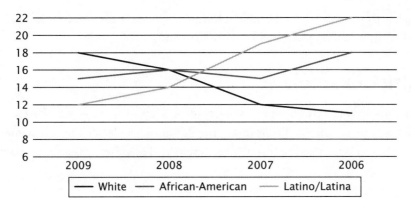

FIGURE 14.4 An example of a time trend chart.

easy-to-follow format so that parents and teachers can gain understanding. This process, which includes putting results in a district-wide or statewide context, is necessary before presenting the data to the community.

A person with these skills can review the findings, compare them to those from previous years, compare the results with other districts, compare schools within the district, and help to identify areas of concern and areas where progress has been made.

School districts, especially smaller ones, may not have someone on staff with the expertise to review the various types of feedback being collected as part of the monitoring system and make sense of it in a way that can be used to help schools. And someone who regularly coordinates academic assessments might not be the best fit for analyzing nonacademic data or focus group responses. In these cases, districts can seek outside support from regional or state education agencies, research centers, nonprofit organizations, or universities (see Box 14.1).

Even if individual schools have someone who can interpret and prepare the data to share, it's important to have a district-level administrator who can look at trends in

BOX 14.1 Strategic Data Project

The Strategic Data Project (SDP), part of the Center for Education Policy Research at Harvard University, partners with school districts and other organizations to improve how education officials use data. Through its fellowship program, data analysts help school systems better understand their data and use it to make decisions that benefit students. SDP also provides a variety of resources, including case studies and a Strategic Use of Data Rubric to help districts assess how they are currently using data and where they need to improve. More information is available at http://sdp.cepr.harvard.edu.

the data across the district, especially if the goal is to apply for grants or to implement particular intervention programs for more than one school.

District Example

Randi Gibson, formerly the director of student support services for the Oceanside Unified School District in California, provides an example[3] of the role a mid-level administrator plays in sifting through the results and identifying the stories they have to tell.

"Schools get massive amounts of information," Gibson says. "How can we narrow it down, and what is it really telling us?"

When Oceanside schools received their California Healthy Kids Survey (CHKS) results, Gibson would work with administrators and pupil personnel staff at the schools to pick a couple of issues to tackle. Substance abuse and gang activity at the middle and high school were two issues that stood out in their CHKS survey data. Using a tiered approach, the district implemented changes that could benefit all students but that were also intended to address issues among specific groups of students at a higher risk:

- The district hired more counselors at the middle and high school levels to increase the number of adults focusing on nonacademic issues and to serve "as the eyes and ears" of the schools, Gibson says.
- Instead of just suspending students, the district created an after-school intervention program. Instead of serving five days of suspension, students serve two days, and the additional time is replaced with courses on substance abuse. So, instead of just missing school, students are learning better ways to respond to pressure.
- At the elementary school level, the schools have worked more on creating a positive culture and getting every staff member to use consistent terms in speaking with students about behavior expectations and social interaction. The schools have been implementing the "Best Behavior" work of Jeffrey Sprague[4] at the University of Oregon, an expert on implementing positive behavior interventions and supports.

15

Sharing the Monitoring Feedback

Whether it's survey data, focus group responses, or the results of a mapping exercise, a vital component of a monitoring system is sharing the information with educators, parents, students, and sometimes even community members as soon as possible so it can be used to improve school climate for the students who are still in the school.

Most people—especially those in education—have taken surveys at one point or another and never heard anything about the results. They're left wondering how their responses compared to others and whether anyone would do anything with the information collected.

As we mentioned earlier, monitoring isn't just collecting data and storing it in a data warehouse or using it to write scientific journal articles that most parents and teachers might never read. Parents deserve to hear what they said as quickly as possible and to see how their views differed from those of their children, from those of the staff, or from parents at other schools (see Box 15.1).

As part of the *Building Capacity* and *Welcoming Practices* projects, individual reports were prepared for the districts and schools as soon as possible so they could review their data and determine which issues to address.

Jennifer Walters, who served as superintendent of the Escondido Union School District, in California, says it was refreshing to work as part of a research project in which the information was not only shared, but also shared in a timely way.

"From the very beginning, it wasn't something being done to the district, but really some common work," Walters said.[1] "Not only would the data information be shared with me or be discussed with us and move our organization forward, but then in updated communications, it was 'here's what we're doing in Washington, here's what we're doing with the coalition.' Other times I've worked with universities, they'll come

---

BOX 15.1 Steps for Sharing the Feedback

- Decide who will be reading the reports on the data.
- If it's a group representing the whole district, the data should focus on the district. But if it's a school, the data should focus more on the school, with some comparison to the district.
- Decide whether data should be presented on all students or separated into subgroups.

---

in and they want to do some research or an investigation. They'll do that and then I have no idea to what extent it's used afterward."

Consider the Audience

Administrators should first consider who will be receiving the information as part of preparing how the information will be released. Parents with school-aged children are constantly juggling work and family life, and teachers often work well into the evening writing lesson plans and grading papers, so giving them a long report that may or may not reflect what is happening in their own school means they might not give it a lot of attention.

One method for informing teachers, parents, policymakers, and members of the public on the results of monitoring surveys is to provide a brief executive summary and then include information on where they can find more details on the results if they are interested. It's important to have the reports reviewed or edited by a communications department or someone who writes for parent audiences.

Focusing on just a few issues is probably a more successful way to get students, parents, and staff members to review or discuss the feedback, especially if they participated in sharing their knowledge or opinions. Engaging students around data can also be done as part of a class or extracurricular project.

Scheduling Time

Part of preparing to share data is having a dedicated time set aside to examine the various pieces of information and plan ways to intervene. If these sessions are integrated into staff members' regular schedule, then monitoring is more likely to become part of the school culture instead of feeling like one more thing they have to do.

Administrators can address data on social and behavioral issues in the same way they do academic goals and needs—through collaborative groups such as professional learning communities or grade-level teams. These collaboration times should have an agenda and a facilitator and should stay focused on the topic.

Create Indices

Again, considering the limited time most people have to review the results of a detailed survey, creating an index is a technique for presenting overall trends in the findings. In an index, several items related to a particular topic—such as whether students feel that adults at school care about them—can be combined.

An index is a way to present a summary of several individual items. It can also be a more reliable presentation of the data, so that it is useful for comparing classrooms, schools, and districts.

Controlling the Results

It's important to note again that just because district leaders support the monitoring concept and have worked to prepare the information in an understandable format doesn't mean that principals, teachers, or parents are comfortable with the information being public—especially if it points to troubling information about student behavior.

There is still tremendous anxiety in some school districts over how data will be perceived if it's released to teachers, parents, or other community members. In fact, sometimes there is an opinion that publicizing a school's data does more harm than good.

There is fear about whether findings indicating the presence of weapons, drug use, or other negative and risky behavior patterns among students might be used to label schools as unsafe or have other damaging consequences for students and staff—even though schools have been required to report such data as part of the now defunct No Child Left Behind program. District leaders have been known to keep the results under wraps, maybe sharing it with just area supervisors or principals, or perhaps downplay the negative trends while highlighting positive results.

Efforts to conceal data on weapons or drugs, however, can backfire if an incident happens that somehow attracts police or media attention. Reporters will only dig deeper using open records requests, thus leaving an impression—whether it's accurate or not— that perhaps the district or school wasn't doing all it could to prevent the incident.

On the other hand, school leaders who stand up and talk in their communities about trends in the data and how they are working with other agencies and providers to try to address problem areas are more likely to earn respect and may even find themselves working with members of the media as partners in tackling the challenges.

Another legitimate fear that educators possess is that, after sharing data for a period of time, the results might not improve or may even get worse. Or, what if a district is using a variety of prevention programs and has relationships with law enforcement officials and other local agencies, but an act of violence still occurs. How then will the community react? Was all of the district's work in vain?

If surveys don't indicate improvement over time—or if one incident seems to upset all the work that has been done to try to protect students—educators should take another look at the strategies they have in place and decide where changes need to be made. Programs and practices should never be implemented in schools and then just left alone, especially those that are meant to address students' social, emotional, and moral development. The environment in which children are growing up is constantly changing. Responses, therefore, need to change and evolve as well. Accepting this attitude and being honest about adjustments that need to be made is a wiser approach than defending existing—possibly ineffective—programs or trying to lay the blame for students' problems elsewhere.

To make another comparison to academic data, teachers and administrators have increasingly adopted the view that achievement data can help them target students' specific needs and better plan their instruction and intervention efforts. The same approach needs to be taken toward nonacademic data, such as information about the social and emotional development of students. Identifying skill trends and needs among students puts schools and districts in a position to take advantage of grants and other funding opportunities. Following the data lets schools know whether they're meeting their goals.

A Measured Approach

It's important to create buy-in for a monitoring system among principals and other school-level staff members, and one way to do that is to avoid sharing the data in a way that ranks schools based on data about weapons, drugs, or other unsafe conditions. While principals, staff members, parents, and students should know what is taking place in their schools, listing schools from top to bottom as an attempt to hold them accountable is not productive.

Amanda Datnow of the University of California San Diego[2] writes about how administrators in one of the districts she has studied urge teachers not to view academic data as a judgment against their own effectiveness. Knowing that data could be used to discuss what is and isn't working well was a key to getting teacher buy-in: "[t]he framing of data use in a collective, less personal way served as an affordance to gaining teacher support in numerous instances," she writes.

It's also important to give educators a chance to get comfortable with examining data before any consequences are attached. Just as a school district might roll out a new assessment system on a pilot basis without high stakes attached for students—such as promotion or remediation—so can a district stay away from labeling a school with problems.

The data collected in youth risk and behavior surveys, for example, are so complex—and often involve so many factors both in and out of school—that to boil all that information down into some sort of score for individual schools is a misguided approach. District leaders might end up removing a principal based on poor outcomes without considering the myriad factors that might explain students' behavior. Other solutions might be more effective, such as bringing in tutors, working with community agencies or police departments to improve neighborhood safety, and offering to students more or better after-school options that are engaging but that also reinforce academic skills.

Data should push educators and other partners to think about solutions and to organize schools to meet the needs of students—not to fear for their jobs.

16

Using Monitoring to Support and Improve Schools

The ultimate goal of implementing a monitoring system is to improve the settings in which children go to school every day and to identify areas where students need support.

Identifying Strengths and Challenges

Data can show which aspects of school climate are already creating positive experiences for students while also leading educators to focus on those areas that need attention or intervention.

Focusing on Vulnerable Populations

Educators should pay special attention to groups of students that might be more likely to exhibit risky behavior or to be victimized by other students. For example, using the California Healthy Kids Survey (CHKS) data, it became clear that military-connected students who have changed schools multiple times experience victimization and reported higher rates of weapon-carrying than others.[1] The schools, therefore, have implemented a wide range of initiatives to help new students feel welcome, meet other students, and get involved in school activities. Similarly, data showing that foster care and homeless youth experience social-emotional difficulties may prompt districts to pay attention to these groups of students and mobilize community and state resources to respond to their needs.

Focusing on Places and Times

Sometimes the data will show that certain incidents among students are more likely to occur during certain times of the school day or in certain areas of the campus, mostly where there is a lack of supervision by adults. This knowledge can help school leaders and students develop innovative solutions for avoiding those problems.

Such a situation[2] took place at Santa Margarita Elementary School—located on Marine Corps Base Camp Pendleton—where tensions among students often boiled over on the playground during recess. Then-Principal Pat Kurtz worked with her playground "duty supervisors" to implement a variety of strategies that would make recess time less stressful and empower both the students and the supervisors to create more positive experiences for students:

- First, when Kurtz brought a child into her office because of a behavior problem, she also brought in the duty supervisor, who likely intervened in the situation on the playground, so that he or she could learn how Kurtz worked with a child who was struggling with peers. Her goal was to show these employees "how you can interact with a child in a positive way that is going to foster their growth instead of punishing them." The practice also sent the students a message that these staff members are part of the school's leadership and have authority.
- Second, through the Peaceful Playgrounds program—which focuses on how to make the best use of recess time and space—the supervisors were also encouraged to have as much playground equipment and games available as possible to avoid situations where students are competing for limited supplies.
- Third, Kurtz worked to foster relationships between the duty supervisors and students. If a student was having a particularly tough time, he or she was assigned a "duty buddy" to check in with the student throughout the day for as long as it took the student to connect with other students in a more positive way.
- Fourth, the lunch/recess time was flipped so that students would play before they eat lunch. If conflicts arose, Kurtz says, they are more eager to resolve them so they could go eat.
- Finally, Kurtz and her staff also made use of a room just off the playground for students having problems with social interaction. Instead of putting students back in the same situation where they were struggling or bullying other kids, they can go instead to the Lunch Recess Options (LRO) room, which is filled with computers, games, art supplies, Legos, and other materials that students can use if the playground is a troublesome place for them that day. Some students also use the room, which is supervised, to complete homework. Certain students also receive priority to use that room because it has been recommended by their teachers or by the school's special education teacher.

Kurtz says she understands that children who are hurting others are probably "just trying to take care of themselves. They just need to find a better way."

Identifying Needs and Matching Resources

When school leaders think they have found a behavior or socio-emotional challenge or need among students that they want to address, their next move is to usually find an "evidence-based" intervention or prevention program that has been piloted in some sample of schools. Districts and schools are often pushed in this direction by state or federal agencies that will only allow funds to be spent on certain approved programs.

But, on its own, an intervention program is insufficient. The process must also involve gathering ongoing feedback from students, parents, teachers, and pupil personnel on how the program is being implemented and whether adjustments are needed to ensure that it fits the needs of the student population and improves the climate within the school.

Also, just because an intervention program worked in one place, in one type of school—or even in a sample of several schools—doesn't mean that it will provide the results that educators are trying to achieve in their own school. A program that worked in that location a few years ago may no longer be relevant in a different setting with different students. In addition, behavior intervention programs are often delivered and tested in a controlled environment and don't necessarily transfer to a public school setting.

There may also be additional ways for schools to address areas of concern:

- *Using bottom-up, homegrown strategies.* Some of the best ideas come from teachers, parents, counselors, and other school staff members who work with students every day. The power of creative and innovative approaches was demonstrated in the *Building Capacity* and *Welcoming Practices*[3] districts. Because of a lack of evidence-based programs specifically designed for military students in public schools, many of the districts and schools in the consortium developed their own strategies for welcoming new students, supporting them through a parent's deployment, and fostering in them a sense of pride and resilience. See Box 16.1 on Because Nice Matters, a locally developed program designed to create a more caring community.
- *Involving community partners.* Smart school administrators know that they can't fix everything on their own. Children go to school, but they also live in communities, go to parks, hang out in the mall, and have needs outside of school hours. Working with community partners and local government agencies to make programs and services available at the school site—such as after-school or counseling programs—can be a more efficient way of keeping students involved in a positive environment and away from potentially dangerous situations or risky behavior. In addition, if weapons are being brought to school, for example, that also means that they exist where children are spending their time outside of school. Banding together with business and community leaders to address the issue can create safer neighborhoods.

- *Referring students and families to resources in the community.* Those same relationships with community leaders and program providers can help when students need support or positive experiences outside of school. Recreation programs, internships or performing arts programs, for example, can be made available to students through partnerships that educators create with a wide variety of individuals and organizations. While many parents are knowledgeable and equipped on their own to seek out these opportunities for their children, schools can be instrumental in making sure that those students with the greatest needs are not left out. An example of such support is the Welconnect app[4] that allows parents to search for resources in the school, district, and community using a very simple app designed for their particular community.

- *Professional development for staff.* Sometimes schools don't need to bring in a program; they need to better train teachers and other staff members to recognize problem behaviors and develop strategies for addressing them. For example, in 2012, an incident occurred on a school bus in a New York town that attracted national attention. In a YouTube video,[5] students were shown harassing an older woman whose job it was to keep order on the bus. In the media, discussions focused on how middle school students could be so cruel and how they should be punished. But perhaps a more important question should have been whether the district was doing anything to train its bus monitors and to set expectations for behavior on the bus. Sometimes the staff members with the least training spend the most time with students during those times when behavior problems can escalate.

- *Involving parents.* Schools rely on parents for support in many areas, but are perhaps underutilizing parents in the area of improving school climate and behavior. Parent volunteers can also be involved in watching the interaction of students in common areas and reinforcing behavior expectations. A 2001 study[6] by researchers at Johns Hopkins University showed that stronger partnerships between schools and parents contribute to better student discipline. Specifically, schools that improved their partnership programs reported lower percentages of students being sent to the principal's office, receiving detention, and receiving in-school suspension. Making sure parents had plenty of opportunities to understand the behavior expectations for their children at school was one approach described in the study. But schools with fewer discipline referrals also recruited community and parent volunteers to help monitor students' behavior at school.

"These findings provide encouraging evidence that the development of quality school, family, and community partnership programs, and the implementation of partnership activities targeted at improving behavior can help reduce the need for disciplinary actions with students," the authors wrote. "By implementing family and community involvement activities to support good student behavior, teachers and administrators may be able to focus more time and effort on student learning and less on behavior management."

BOX 16.1 Because Nice Matters

Using data to reduce bullying and improve school climate should involve analysis of outcomes and trends, but it should also be combined with what feels right in a school. That's the approach the Temecula Valley Unified School District in California has taken with "Because Nice Matters"—a grass-roots initiative informed by Great Oak High School Assistant Principal Judy Stapleton's years of experience working with students.[9]

The program encourages and recognizes kind behavior and involves symbolic activities, such as wearing purple and black to remind everyone that bullying can cause physical and psychological damage or wearing white to signify making a fresh start. Painting a large school bus with the slogan was also an eye-catching way to make the statement. Stapleton created a "bully incident report" for students to report not only when bullying happens to them, but also when they witness it happening.

Once the program was in place, Stapleton began to track suspension and expulsion data related to bullying, including fights, "over-the-top horseplay," and threats.

Even though enrollment in the district is growing, incidents related to bullying behavior have been dropping since "Because Nice Matters" began.

"[The trends are] moving in the right direction," Stapleton says. "Typically with the growth of population the incidents should also grow. This tells me that our proactive program is making an impact."

Stapleton and other staff in the district also attended workshops organized by the *Building Capacity* project at the University of Southern California (USC), and learned about risk factors affecting students in military families. This provided educators with additional tools to strengthen their anti-bullying efforts. Now the district is implementing "Because Nice Matters" throughout the system and collecting additional data to measure the program's effectiveness.

"I have seen a big increase in students reporting bullying on behalf of others, which is very encouraging as there are way more witnesses than victims and bullies," Stapleton says. "The two-pronged approach—saying no to bullying and being nice to others and keeping it alive all year long is making a difference."

Involving Students in Understanding Data

Even at the elementary level, students have become increasingly involved in tracking their own academic progress. They can also be included in efforts to understand data on issues of safety, behavior, and the overall climate of their schools.

The Council for Youth Research at the University of California Los Angeles (UCLA)[7] is a participatory research model being implemented in South and East Los Angeles through the Institute for Democracy, Education and Access (IDEA) at UCLA. The Council brings high school students together to examine and use data to improve educational conditions and equity within their schools. Called *youth participatory action research*, the project "combines dimensions of academic learning with civic learning," says Dr. John Rogers, an associate professor of education at UCLA and the director of IDEA. "Both are important."

The Council began more than a decade ago as part of a summer seminar and then developed into an extracurricular club led by teacher/facilitators who "want to have meaningful, sustained relationships with young people," Rogers says. Some middle school teachers have also integrated similar research and advocacy projects into their curriculum.

Creating PowerPoint presentations, videos, and other media to present their findings, the students address topics such as the causes of dropping out, access to technology in their schools, and whether students feel their teachers care about them. They have had opportunities to share their research with both education and government leaders in Los Angeles.

The Council brings together a diverse mix of students, both in their achievement levels and in their views on various topics. "We want multiple perspectives," Rogers said,[8] adding that when the students work together, "it's hard to tell who the A student is. Anecdotally, some of the students have gone on to elite colleges and done well because of this kind of experience."

The challenge of presenting information in constructive, positive ways is not something unique to researchers; the students wrestle with this as well. Students feel empowered by sharing their data, Rogers says, but the facilitators also encourage people to share the information "in ways that won't shut people down."

There have been cases when school administrators have reacted defensively to the information being presented, but some school leaders have also used the students' data to change policies or procedures. In one case, a principal changed how students were assigned to counselors after the Council presented information showing that some students were not having their needs addressed by counselors.

For an initiative such as the Council to be effective, school officials and policymakers need to change how they view and include students' perspectives in the way schools operate, Rogers says.

"There is a tendency for urban high schools to emphasize top-down control around knowledge and behavior," he says. "This sort of activity is bound to create problems unless you re-culture what schools are about."

Conclusion

Implications for the Future

Currently, as this book is being written, there is a national trend toward integrating social-emotional learning (SEL) and positive school climates into the academic mission of the school. The Every Student Succeeds Act (ESSA); the Aspen Institute's National Commission on Social, Emotional, and Academic Development; the National Center on School Climate; the Collaborative for Academic, Social, and Emotional Learning; and other organizations have put forth strong policy, research, and practice agendas to include these important variables as a focus of K-12 schooling in the United States and worldwide. The authors of this guide aim to extend this effort to more school systems around the world, and the examples included here support this national and international effort.

The ideas and practices presented in this guide, however, go beyond a specific point in history. The assumptions and values underlying supportive school monitoring are central to the educational mission of schools. Supportive monitoring is democratic and empowering for all school constituencies. Listening to the voices of students, parents, and staff, sharing what has been heard, and acting upon it reflect a democratic process. Supportive school monitoring can make this democratic process an ordinary magic, performed every day in schools as part of ongoing practice.

The focus on each individual school and providing opportunities to tailor-fit the supportive monitoring system—or at least significant parts of this system—to each school's needs is a remedy against "one-size-fits-all" solutions. It helps the school discover and maintain its uniqueness without rejecting accountability altogether. By making supportive monitoring an integral part of school life, accountability systems are not an oppressive outside intervention in the school. Instead, they are a path toward responsible and responsive education that is based on values and data-driven at the same time.

Educators teach students about the importance of data in making key decisions. They encourage students to look for the most accurate data and take advantage of it. Sadly, however, many school administrators and teachers dread data, mainly because it's been used to punish schools and teachers. It has become associated with punitive external surveillance aimed at schools struggling to educate students in urban settings with grossly insufficient resources due to inequality. Supportive monitoring presents an alternative that works in conjunction with SEL, school climate measures, and evidence-based programs. It is a process and infrastructure that leverages data to help improve the school and to identify populations and needs that may actually help bring resources to the school. Systematic and reliable data can help document needs and enable educators to apply for relevant grants that can help turn schools around.

Schools need not go it alone. While the authors emphasize the importance of localizing the monitoring process, ideally, schools would be part of a larger district- and national-level supportive monitoring system. These larger systems can support individual schools by providing expertise, technology, and other resources so that schools with fewer resources can develop their own site-level monitoring systems. Such a supportive infrastructure could be built state by state or even nationally and still allow local autonomy, creativity, adaptability, and transferability.

Finally, this guide describes ways that supportive school monitoring can help schools and districts. Local knowledge can accumulate for the benefit of all. Imagine the power when millions of student, parent, and teacher voices are aggregated and amplified through policy, research, and media in depth. Today's technologies provide the means to mine all these rich data sources accumulating across the nation and over time. Analyzing this big but democratic and ground-up data could focus, for instance, on schools across the nation that "beat the odds" and do much better than anyone could expect based on their demographics. Much can be learned from these schools, identified by the large-scale aggregation of data.

As we said in the introduction, each district is different, and the schools within each district each have unique needs and strengths. From a district-wide perspective, monitoring and mapping allow educators to address concerns that affect multiple schools or groups of students across multiple schools, while also focusing on bullying behavior, patterns of violence, or areas of risk at a single school.

These methods involve all members of the school community—especially the students—in providing ongoing information on their experiences before, during, and after the school day. When collected on a regular basis, the perceptions of students, staff members, and even parents can be a source of empowerment, democracy, voice, and, at the same time, a reliable source of data on the areas of risk within and surrounding a campus.

Appendix

The following is a list of scholarly references related to monitoring.

Astor, R. A., Benbenishty, R., Marachi, R., & Meyer, H. A. (2006). The social context of schools: Monitoring and mapping student victimization in schools. In S. Jimerson & M. J. Furlong (Eds.), *Handbook of school violence and school safety: From research to practice* (pp. 221–233). Mahwah, NJ: Erlbaum.

Astor, R. A., Benbenishty, R., & Meyer, H. A. (2004). Monitoring and mapping student victimization in schools. *Theory Into Practice, 43(1)*, 39–49.

Astor, R. A., Benbenishty, R., Shadmy, H., Raz, T., Algersy, E., Zeharia, M., . . . De Pedro, K. (2011). No school left behind: merging Israel's national academic and school safety monitoring system and matching data-driven interventions for each school. In J. S. Hoffman, L. Knox, & R. Cohen (Eds.), *Beyond suppression: Global perspectives on youth violence* (chapter 8). Part of Global Crime and Justice series; Graeme R. Newman, Series Editor. Santa Barbara, CA: Praeger.

Astor, R. A., Capp, G. Moore, H., & Benbenishty, R. (in press, 2016). Lessons from monitoring social emotional learning in Israel and California schools. In R. H. Shute & P. T. Slee (Eds.), *Mental health through schools: The way forward*. Hove: Routledge.

Benbenishty, R., & Astor, R. A. (2005). School violence in context: Culture, neighborhood, family, school, and gender. New York: Oxford University Press.

Benbenishty, R., & Astor, R. A. (2007). Monitoring indicators of children's victimization in school: Linking national-, regional-, and site-level indicators. *Social Indicators Research.* 84(3), 333–348.

Benbenishty, R., & Astor, R. A. (2012). Monitoring school violence in Israel. National studies and beyond: Implications for theory, practice, and policy. In S. R. Jimerson, A. B. Nickerson, M. J. Mayer, & M. J. Furlong (Eds.), *Handbook of school violence and school safety: International research and practice*, 2nd ed. (pp. 191–202). New York: Routledge.

Benbenishty, R., & Astor, R. A. (in progress for 2018). The scientific basis and method of monitoring for school safety and empowerment.

Benbenishty, R., Astor, R. A., Shadmy, H., Luk, A., & Glickman, H. (in progress for 2018). Reducing school violence and bullying using monitoring and policy: The Israel Model.

Benbenishty, R., Astor, R. A., & Zeira, A. (2003). Monitoring school violence: Linking, national-, district-, and school-level data over time. *Journal of School Violence, 2(2)*, 29–50.

Pitner, R., Moore, H., Capp, G., Iachini, A. L., Berkowitz, R., Benbenishty, R., & Astor, R. A. (2017). School safety, victimization, and bullying: An overview of violence interventions and monitoring approaches. In C. Franklin (Ed.), *Encyclopedia of social work online* (ESWO). New York: Oxford University Press.

Notes

INTRODUCTION

1. https://www.cdc.gov/violenceprevention/youthviolence/index.html
   https://www.nasponline.org/resources-and-publications/resources/school-safety-and-crisis/school-violence-prevention
   http://www.cctatr.com/a
2. Astor, R. A., Jacobson, L., Benbenishty, R., Atuel, H., Gilreath, T., Wong, M., De Pedro, K. M., Esqueda, M. C., & Estrada, J. N. (2012). A school administrator's guide to creating supportive schools for military students. New York: Columbia University, Teachers College Press.

   Benbenishty, R., & Astor, R. A. (2012). Monitoring school violence in Israel, National studies and beyond: Implications for theory, practice, and policy. In S. R. Jimerson, A.B. Nickerson, M.J. Mayer & M. J. Furlong (Eds.), *Handbook of school violence and school safety: International research and practice. Second Edition* (pp. 191–202). New York: Routledge.
3. http://www.casel.org/; http://www.schoolclimate.org/
4. https://www.cdc.gov/surveillancepractice/
5. https://www.cdc.gov/healthyyouth/data/yrbs/index.htm

CHAPTER 1

1. http://www.fairtest.org
2. https://www2.ed.gov/policy/elsec/leg/essa/index.html

CHAPTER 2

1. http://cal-schls.wested.org/
2. https://buildingcapacity.usc.edu/

CHAPTER 4

1. Denham, 2015.
2. http://www.ilcommunityschools.org/images/files/docs/Community%20Asset%20Mapping%20-%20Overview%20%26%20Resource%20Assessment.pdf

CHAPTER 5

1. http://www.gatesfoundation.org/media-center/press-releases/2013/01/measures-of-effective-teaching-project-releases-final-research-report

2. https://dese.mo.gov/sites/default/files/Hanover-Research-Student-Surveys.pdf
3. http://journals.sagepub.com/doi/abs/10.1177/0044118X10388219

CHAPTER 6

1. Vanderbilt Assessment of Leadership in Education http://valed.discoveryeducation.com/
2. Teaching, Empowering, Leading, and Learning (TELL) survey https://newteachercenter.org/approach/teaching-empowering-leading-and-learning-tell/

CHAPTER 8

1. http://cahnrs.wsu.edu/fs/wp-content/uploads/sites/4/2015/09/A-Step-By-Step-Guide-to-Developing-Effective-Questionnaires.pdf
2. For a detailed presentation and examples, see http://oprs.usc.edu/education/informed-consent/

CHAPTER 9

1. The reader may want to consult a basic textbook on focus groups, such as:
   Krueger, A., & Casey, M. A. (2015). *Focus groups: A practical guide for applied research*. Sage, Los Angeles.

CHAPTER 10

1. Astor, R. A., Meyer, H. A., & Behre, W. J. (1999). Unowned places and times: Maps and interviews about violence in high schools. *American Educational Research Journal, 36*, 3–42.
2. Based on a personal interview with a school representative.
3. http://www.wakeed.org/wp-content/uploads/2014/04/54562.pdf
4. Based on a personal interview.

CHAPTER 11

1. For detailed discussions see Astor, R. A., Meyer, H. A., & Behre, W. J. (1999). Unowned places and times: Maps and interviews about violence in high schools. *American Educational Research Journal, 36*, 3–42; Astor, R. A., Meyer, H. A., & Pitner, R. O. (2001). Elementary and middle school students' perceptions of violence-prone school sub-contexts. *The Elementary School Journal, 101*(5), 511–528; and Astor, R. A., Benbenishty, R., & Meyer, H. A. (2004). Monitoring and mapping student victimization in schools. *Theory Into Practice, 43*(1), 39–49.
2. https://www.ncbi.nlm.nih.gov/pubmed/25620449

CHAPTER 12

1. https://www.pbisapps.org/Pages/Default.aspx
2. McIntosh, K., Campbell, A. L., Carter, D. R., & Zumbo, B. D. (2009). Concurrent validity of office discipline referrals and cut points used in schoolwide positive behavior support. *Behavioral Disorders, 34*, 100–113; and Nelson, J. R., Benner, G. J., Reid, R. C., Epstein, M. H., & Currin, D. (2002). The convergent validity of office discipline referrals with the CBCL-TRF. *Journal of Emotional and Behavioral Disorders, 10*, 181–188.
3. https://partnerdashboard.cps-k12.org/strive/
4. https://sowkweb.usc.edu/news/military-schools-project-supports-peer-learning-program
5. https://sowkweb.usc.edu/news/military-schools-project-supports-peer-learning-program

CHAPTER 13

1. http://cyberbullying.org/schools-monitor-students-social-media-accounts
2. For innovative ways to use Twitter in class, visit http://www.edudemic.com/the-30-newest-ways-to-use-twitter-in-the-classroom/

3. https://www.facebook.com/safety/groups/teachers/

4. https://www.youtube.com/watch?v=Cnb2SnVRO6Y

5. http://www.ajaproject.org/

6. https://photovoice.org/

7. https://coms.publishpath.com/Websites/coms/Files/Content/963915/Strack%20et%20al.%20photovoice.pdf

8. Interview.

9. http://www.edudemic.com/the-30-newest-ways-to-use-twitter-in-the-classroom/

CHAPTER 14

1. http://sdp.cepr.harvard.edu/fellowship

2. http://sdp.cepr.harvard.edu/rubric

3. Interview.

4. http://www.voyagersopris.com/curriculum/subject/school-climate/best-behavior/overview

CHAPTER 15

1. Interview.

2. http://journals.sagepub.com/doi/abs/10.1177/0044118X10388219

CHAPTER 16

1. Gilreath, T. D., Astor, R. A., Cederbaum, J. A., Atuel, H., & Benbenishty, R. (2013). Prevalence and correlates of victimization and weapon carrying among military- and nonmilitary- connected youth in Southern California. *Preventive Medicine*, http://dx.doi.org/10.1016/j.ypmed.2013.12.002

2. Interview.

3. https://buildingcapacity.usc.edu

4. Welconnect.org.

5. https://www.youtube.com/watch?v=l93wAqnPQwk

6. http://spdg.ctserc.com/assets/improving%20student%20behavior%20and%20school%20discipline%20with%20family%20and%20community%20involvement.pdf

7. https://idea.gseis.ucla.edu/projects/the-council-of-youth-research

8. Interview.

9. http://www.tvusd.k12.ca.us/BecauseNiceMattersWeek

Index

Page numbers followed by *b*, *f*, or *t* indicate boxes, figures, or tables, respectively. Numbers followed by n indicate notes.